The Battle of New Orleans

The Battle of
New Orleans

Zachary F. Smith

LEONAUR

The Battle of New Orleans
by Zachary F. Smith

Originally published under the title:
*The Battle of New Orleans: Including the Previous Engagements
Between The Americans and the British, the Indians, and the Spanish
Which Led to the Final Conflict on the 8th Of January, 1815*

Leonaur is an imprint of Oakpast Ltd

ISBN: 978-1-84677-676-2 (hardcover)
ISBN: 978-1-84677-675-6 (softcover)

http://www.leonaur.com

Publisher's Notes

Contents

Preface

In the preparation of the following account of the Battle of New Orleans, I have availed myself of all accessible authorities, and have been placed under obligations to Colonel R. T. Durrett, of Louisville, Kentucky. I have had free access to his library, which is the largest private collection in this country, and embraces works upon almost every subject. Besides general histories of the United States and of the individual States, and periodicals, newspapers, and manuscripts, which contain valuable information on the Battle of New Orleans, his library contains numerous works more specifically devoted to this subject. Among these, to which I have had access, may be mentioned *Notices of the War of 1812*, by John M. Armstrong, two volumes, New York, 1840; *The Naval History of Great Britain from 1783 to 1830*, by Edward P. Brenton, two volumes, London, 1834; *History of the Late War*, by H.M. Brackenridge, Philadelphia, 1839; *An Authentic History of the Second War for Independence*, by Samuel R. Brown, two volumes, Auburn, 1815; *History of the Late War by an American* (Joseph Cushing), Baltimore, 1816; *Correspondence Between General Jackson and General Adair as to the Kentuckians Charged by Jackson With Inglorious Flight*, New Orleans, 1815; *An Authentic History of the Late War*, by Paris M. Davis, New York,

1836; *A Narrative of the Campaigns of the British Army* by an Officer (George R. Gleig), Philadelphia, 1821; *History of Louisiana, American Dominion*, by Charles Gayarre, New York, 1866; *The Second War with England*, illustrated, by J.T. Headley, two volumes, New York, 1853; *History of the War of 1812 Between the United States and Great Britain*, by Rossiter Johnson, New York, 1882; *The Pictorial Field-Book of the War of 1812*, by Benjamin J. Lossing, New York, 1868; *The War of 1812 in the Western Country*, by Robert B. McAfee, Lexington, Kentucky, 1816; *Historical Memoirs of the War of 1814-1815*, by Major A. Lacarriere Latour, Philadelphia, 1816; *Messages of James Madison, President of the United States, Parts One and Two*, Albany, 1814; *The Military Heroes of the War of 1812*, by Charles J. Peterson, Philadelphia, 1858; *The Naval War of 1812*, by Theodore Roosevelt, New York, 1889; *The History of the War of 1812-15*, by J. Russell, junior, Hartford, 1815; *The Glory of America*, etc., by R. Thomas, New York, 1834; *Historic Sketches of the Late War*, by John L. Thomson, Philadelphia, 1816; *The Life of Andrew Jackson*, by Alexander Walker, Philadelphia, 1867; *A Full and a Correct Account of the Military Occurrences of the Late War Between Great Britain and the United States*, by James Williams, two volumes, London, 1818.

I have also been placed under obligations to Mr. William Beer, librarian of the Howard Library of New Orleans, which has become a depository of rare works touching the history of the South Mississippi Valley, and especially relating to the War of 1812 and the Battle of New Orleans. A list of all the works in this library which Mr. Beer placed at my disposal would be too long for insertion here, but the following may be mentioned: Claiborne's *Notes on the War in the South*, Goodwin's *Biography of Andrew Jackson*, Reid and Easten's *Life of General Jackson*, Nolte's *Fifty Years in Both Hemispheres, Report of Committee on Jackson's War-*

rant for Closing the Halls of the Legislature of Louisiana, The Madison Papers, Ingersoll's *Historic Sketch of the Second War Between Great Britain and the United States,* Cooke's *Seven Campaigns in the Peninsula.* Hill's *Recollections of an Artillery Officer,* Coke's *History of the Rifle Brigade, Diary of Private Timewell,* and Cooke's *Narrative of Events.* No one would do justice to himself or his subject if he should write a history of the battle of New Orleans without availing himself of the treasures of the Howard Library.

Z. F. Smith

Introduction

England was apparently more liberal than Spain or France when, in the treaty of 1783, she agreed to the Mississippi River as the western boundary of the United States. Spain was for limiting the territory of the new republic on the west to the crest of the Alleghany Mountains, so as to secure to her the opportunity of conquering from England the territory between the mountains and the Great River. Strangely enough and inconsistently enough, France supported Spain in this outrageous effort to curtail the territory of the new republic after she had helped the United States to conquer it from England, or rather after General Clark had wrested it from England for the colony of Virginia, and while Virginia was still in possession of it. The seeming liberality of England, however, may not have been more disinterested than the scheming of Spain and France in this affair. England did not believe that the United States could exist as a permanent government, but that the confederated States would disintegrate and return to her as colonies. The King of England said as much when the treaty was made. If, then, the States were to return to England as colonies, the more territory they might bring with them the better, and hence a large grant was acknowledged in the treaty of peace. The acts of England toward the United States after acknowledging their independence indicate that the fixing of the western boundary on the Mississippi had as much selfishness as liberality, if indeed it was not entirely selfish.

The ink was scarcely dry upon the parchment which bore evidence of the ratified treaty of 1783 when the mother country began acts of hostility and meanness against her children who had separated from her and begun a political life for themselves. When the English ships of war, which had blockaded New York for seven long years, sailed out of the harbour and took their course toward the British Isles, instead of hauling down their colours from the flagstaff of Fort George, they left them flying over the fortification, and tried to prevent them from being removed by chopping down all the cleats for ascent, and greasing the pole so that no one could climb to the top and pull down the British flag or replace it by the colours of the United States. An agile sailor boy, named Van Arsdale, who had probably ascended many trees in search of bird's nests, and clambered up the masts of ships until he had become an expert climber, nailed new cleats to the flagstaff and climbed to its summit, bearing with him the flag of the new republic. When he reached the top he cut down the British flag and suspended that of the United States. This greasy trick may have been the act of some wag of the retiring fleet, and might have been taken for a joke had it not been followed by hostile acts which indicated that this was the initial step in a long course of hostility and meanness.

But it was soon followed by the retention of the lake forts which fell into British hands during the Revolutionary War, and which, by the terms of the treaty, were to be surrendered. Instead of surrendering them according to the stipulations of the treaty, they held them, and not only occupied them for thirteen years, but used them as storehouses and magazines from which the Indians were fed and clothed and armed and encouraged to tomahawk and scalp Americans without regard to age or sex. And then followed a series of orders in council, by which the commerce of the United States was almost swept from the seas, and their sailors forcibly taken from American ships to serve on British. These orders in council were so frequent that it seemed as if the French on one side of the British Channel and the English on the other were hurling decrees and orders at one another for their own amusement while inflicting dire injuries on other nations, and especially the Americans.

Had it not been for these hostile acts of the British there would have been no War of 1812. Had they continued to treat the young republic with the justice and liberality to which they agreed in fixing its western boundary in the treaty of 1783, no matter what their motive may have been, there would have been no cause for war between the two countries. The Americans had hardly recovered from the wounds inflicted in the Revolutionary War. They were too few and too weak and too poor to go to war with such a power as England, and moreover wanted a continuance of the peace by which they were adding to the population and wealth of their country. What they had acquired in the quarter of a century since the end of the Revolutionary War was but little in comparison with the accumulations of England during long centuries, and they were not anxious to risk their all in a conflict with such a power; but young and weak and few as they were, they belonged to that order of human beings who hold their rights and their honour in such high regard that they can not continuously be insulted and injured without retaliation. The time came when they resolved to bear the burdens of war rather than submit to injustice and dishonour.

In the French and Indian war which preceded the Revolution there was fighting for some time before a formal declaration of war. The English drove the French traders from the Ohio Valley, and the French forced out the English while the two nations were at peace. The French chassed from one of their forts to another with fiddles instead of drums, and the English with fowling-pieces instead of muskets rambled over the forest, but they sometimes met and introduced each other to acts of war while a state of hostility was acknowledged by neither. Something like a similar state of things preceded the War of 1812. Tecumseh was at work trying to unite all the tribes of Indians in one grand confederacy, ostensibly to prevent them from selling their lands to the Americans, but possibly for the purpose of war. While he was at this work his brother, the Prophet, had convinced the Indians that he had induced the Great Spirit to make them bullet-proof, and the English so encouraged them with food and clothing and arms that they believed they were able to conquer the Americans, and began to carry on hostilities against them without any formal declaration of war by either party. The battle of Tippecanoe, which came of this superstition among the Indians and this encouragement from England, may be considered the first clash of arms in the War of 1812. The English took no open or active part in this battle, but their arms and ammunition and rations were in it, and after it was lost the Indians went to the English and became their open allies when the War of 1812 really began. Whether the English were allies of the Indians or the Indians allies of the English, they fought and bled and died and were conquered together after the initial conflict at Tippecanoe, in 1811, to the final battle at New Orleans in 1815, which crowned the American arms with a glory never to fade.

The Filson Club, whose broad field of work in history, literature, science, and art is hardly indicated by the name of the first historian of Kentucky, which it bears, has deemed three of the battles which were fought during the War of

1812 as the most important of the many that were waged. These three were, first, the battle of Tippecanoe, regarded as the opening scene of the bloody drama; second, the battle of the Thames, by which the power of the British was crushed in the west and northwest, and third, the battle of New Orleans, which ended the war in a glorious victory for the Americans. The Club determined to have the history of these three battles written and filed among its archives, and to have the matter published for the benefit of the public. Hence, the task was undertaken by three different members of the Club.

The first of these, "The Battle of Tippecanoe," was prepared for the Club by Captain Alfred Pirtle, and published in 1900 as Filson Club Publication Number 15. It is an illustrated quarto of one hundred and sixty-seven pages, which gives a detailed account of the battle of Tippecanoe and the acts of the Indians and British which led to it and the important consequences which followed. The names of the officers and soldiers, and especially those of Kentucky who were engaged in it, are given so far as could be ascertained, and the book is a historic record of this battle, full enough and faithful enough to furnish the reader with all of the important facts.

The second, "The Battle of the Thames," the 5th of October, 1813, was undertaken by Colonel Bennett H. Young, and appeared in 1903 as the eighteenth publication of the Filson Club. It is an elaborately illustrated quarto of two hundred and eighty-six pages, and presents a detailed account of the acts which led up to the main battle and the engagements by land and water which preceded it. It contains a list of all the Kentuckians who as officers and privates were in the battle. The reader who seeks information about this battle need look no further than its pages.

The third and last of these important battles occurred at

New Orleans the 8th of January, 1815. Its history was prepared for the Club by Mr. Z. F. Smith, and now appears as Filson Club Publication Number Nineteen, for the year 1904. It is an illustrated quarto in the adopted style of the Club, which has been so much admired for its antique paper and beautiful typography. It sets forth with fullness and detail the hostilities which preceded and led to the main battle, and gives such a clear description of the final conflict by the assistance of charts as to enable the reader to understand the manoeuvres of both sides and to virtually see the battle as it progressed from the beginning to the end. This battle ended the War of 1812, and when the odds against the Americans are considered, it must be pronounced one of the greatest victories ever won upon the battlefield. The author, Mr. Z. F. Smith, was an old-line Whig, and was taught to hate Jackson as Henry Clay, the leader of the Whigs, hated him, but he has done the old hero full justice in this narrative, and has assigned him full honours of one of the greatest victories ever won. Although his sympathies were with General Adair, a brother Kentuckian, he takes up the quarrel between him and General Jackson and does Jackson full and impartial justice. If Jackson had been as unprejudiced against Adair as the author against Jackson, there would have been nothing like a stain left upon the escutcheon of the Kentuckians who abandoned the fight on the west bank of the Mississippi because it was their duty to get out of it rather than be slaughtered like dumb brutes who neither see impending danger nor reason about the mistakes of superiors and the consequences. He who reads the account of the battle of New Orleans which follows this introduction will know more about that battle than he knew before, or could have learned from any other source in so small a compass.

R. T. Durrett
President of The Filson Club

CHAPTER 1

The Gulf Coast Campaign

On the 26th of November, 1814, a fleet of sixty great ships weighed anchor, unfurled their sails, and put to sea, as the smoke lifted and floated away from a signal gun aboard the Tonnant, the flagship of Admiral Sir Alexander Cochrane, from Negril Bay, on the coast of Jamaica. Nearly one half of these vessels were formidable warships, the best of the English navy, well divided between line-of-battle ships of sixty-four, seventy-four, and eighty guns, frigates of forty to fifty guns, and sloops and brigs of twenty to thirty guns each. In all, one thousand pieces of artillery mounted upon the decks of these frowned grimly through as many port-holes, bidding defiance to the navies of the world and safely convoying over thirty transports and provisioning ships, bearing every equipment for siege or battle by sea and for a formidable invasion of an enemy's country by land. Admiral Cochrane, in chief command, and Admiral Malcombe, second in command, were veteran officers whose services and fame are a part of English history.

On board of this fleet was an army and its retinue, computed by good authorities to number fourteen thousand men, made up mainly of the veteran troops of the British military forces recently operating in Spain and France, trained in the campaigns and battles against Napoleon through years of war, and victors in the end in these contests. Major Latour, Chief Engineer of General Jackson's army, in his "Memoirs of the War in Florida and Louisiana in 1814-15," has carefully compiled from British official sources a detailed statement of the regiments, corps, and companies which constituted the army of invasion under Pakenham, at New Orleans, as follows:

Fourth Regiment— King's Own	Lieutenant-Colonel Brooks	750
Seventh Regiment— Royal Fusiliers	Lieutenant-Colonel Blakeney	850
Fourteenth Regiment— Duchess of York's Own	Lieutenant-Colonel Baker	350
Twenty-first Regiment— Royal Fusiliers	Lieutenant-Colonel Patterson	900
Fortieth Regiment— Somersetshire	Lieutenant-Colonel H. Thornton	1,000
Forty-third Regiment— Monmouth Light Infantry	Lieutenant-Colonel Patrickson	850
Forty-fourth Regiment— East Essex	Lieutenant-Colonel Mullen	750
Eighty-fifth Regiment— Buck Volunteers	Lieutenant-Colonel Wm. Thornton	650
Ninety-third Regiment— Highlanders	Lieutenant-Colonel Dale	1,100
Ninety-fifth Regiment— Rifle Corps	Major Mitchell	500
First Regiment— West India (coloured)	Lieutenant-Colonel Whitby	700
Fifth Regiment— West India (coloured)	Lieutenant-Colonel Hamilton	700
A detachment from the Sixty-second Regiment		350
Rocket Brigade, Artillery, Engineers, Sappers and Miners		1,500
Royal Marines and sailors from the fleet		3,500
	Total	14,450

Including artillerists, marines, and others, seamen of the ships' crews afloat, there were not fewer than eighteen thousand men, veterans in the service of their country in the lines of their respective callings, to complete the equipment of this powerful armada.

At the head of this formidable army of invasion were Lord Edward Pakenham, commander-in-chief; Major-General Samuel Gibbs, commanding the first, Major-General John Lambert, the second, and Major-General John Keene, the third divisions, supported by subordinate officers, than whom none living were braver or more skilled in the science and practice of war. Nearly all had learned their lessons under the great Wellington, the conqueror of Napoleon. Since 1588, when the combined naval and military forces of England were summoned to repel the attempted invasion and conquest of that country by the Spanish Armada, the British Government had not often fitted out and sent against an enemy a combined armament so powerful and so costly as that which rendezvoused in the tropical waters of Negril Bay in the latter autumn days of 1814. Even the fleet of Nelson at the Battle of the Nile, sixteen years before, where he won victory and immortal honours by the destruction of the formidable French fleet, was far inferior in number of vessels, in ordnance, and in men to that of Admiral Cochrane on this expedition. The combined equipment cost England forty millions of dollars.

In October and November of this year, the marshalling of belligerent forces by sea and land from the shores of Europe and America, with orders to rendezvous at a favourable manoeuvring point in the West Indies, caused much conjecture as to the object in view. That the War Department of the English Government meditated a winter campaign somewhere upon the southern coasts of the United States was a common belief; that an invasion of Louisiana and the capture and occupation of New Orleans was meant, many surmised. For reasons of State policy, the object of the expedition in view was held a secret until the day of setting sail. Now it was disclosed by those in command that New Orleans was the objective point, and officers and men were animated with the hope that, in a few weeks more, they would be quartered for the winter in the subjugated capital of Louisiana, with a dream that the coveted territory might be occupied and permanently held as a possession of the British Empire.

The Government at Washington was advised that, during the summer and early autumn months of 1814, our implacable enemy was engaged in preparations for a renewal of hostilities on a scale of magnitude and activity beyond anything attempted since the war began; but it seemed not fully to interpret the designs and plans of the British leaders. Especially unfortunate, and finally disastrous to the American arms, was the inaptness and inertness of the Secretary of War, General Armstrong, in failing to adopt, promptly and adequately, measures to meet the emergency. For almost a year after the destruction of the English fleet on Lake Erie by Commodore Perry, and of the English army at the battle of the Thames by General Harrison, a period of comparative repose ensued between the belligerents. The British Government was too much absorbed in delivering the *coup-de-main* to the great Napoleon to give attention to America. But her opportunity came. The allied powers defeated and decimated the armies of the French Emperor, and forced him to capitulate in his own capital. On the 3rd of March, 1814, they entered Paris. On the eleventh of May Napoleon abdicated, and was sent an exile to Elba.

England was at peace with all Europe. Her conquering armies and fleets would be idle for an indefinite period; yet, it would be premature to disband the former or to dismantle the latter. Naturally, attention turned to the favourable policy of employing these vast and ready resources for the chastisement and humiliation of her American enemies, as a fit closing of the war and punishment for their rebellious defiance. Under orders, the troops in France and Spain were marched to Bordeaux and placed in a camp of concentration, from which they were debarked in fleets down the river Garonne, and across the Atlantic to their destinations in America. An English officer with these troops expressed the sentiment of the soldiers and seamen, and of the average citizen of England at this time, in this language: "It was the general opinion that a large proportion of the Peninsular army would be transported to the other side of the Atlantic, that the war would there be carried on with vigour, and that no terms of accommodation would be listened to, except such as a British general should dictate in the Republican Senate."

Overtures for the negotiation-of a treaty of peace had been interchanged between the two nations at war as early as January. By April the American Commissioners were in Europe, though the arrival of the English Commissioners at Ghent for final deliberations was delayed until August. Meanwhile, several thousands of these Peninsular troops were transported to reinforce the army in Canada. On the sixteenth of August a small fleet of British vessels in Chesapeake Bay was reinforced by thirty sail under the command of Admirals Cochrane and Malcombe, one half of which were ships of war. A large part of this flotilla moved up the Potomac and disembarked about six thousand men, under command of General Ross. The battle of Bladensburg was fought on the twenty-fourth, followed immediately by the capture of Washington and the burning of the Government buildings there. A few days after, the combined naval and military British forces were defeated in an attack on Baltimore, General Ross, commander-in-chief, being among the slain. About the same date, Commodore McDonough won a great and crushing victory over the English fleet on Lake Champlain, while the British army of fourteen thousand men, under Sir George Prevost, was signally defeated by the Americans, less than seven thousand in number, at Plattsburg, on the border of New York.

Such was the military situation in the first month of autumn, 1814. Seemingly, the British plenipotentiaries had a motive in reserve for delaying the negotiations for peace. England yet looked upon the United States as her wayward prodigal, and conjured many grievances against the young nation that had rebuked her cruel insolence and pride in two wars. She nursed a spirit of imperious and bitter revenge. A London organ, recently before, had said: "In diplomatic circles it is rumoured that our military and naval commanders in America have no power to conclude any armistice or suspension of arms. Terms will be offered to the American Government at the point of the bayonet. America will be left in a much worse situation as a commercial and naval power than she was at the commencement of the war."

The reverses to the British arms on Lake Champlain, at Plattsburg, and at Baltimore, virtually ended hostilities in the Northern States for the remaining period of the war. Winter approaching, all belligerent forces that could be marshalled would be transferred to the waters of the Gulf for operations on the coast there. The malice and wanton barbarity of the English in burning the national buildings and property at Washington, in the destruction and loot of houses, private and public, on the shores of the Chesapeake and Atlantic, and in repeated military outrages unjustified by the laws of civilized warfare, had fully aroused the Government and the citizenship to the adoption of adequate measures of defence for the Northern and Eastern States. It

SEAT OF WAR IN LOUISIANA & FLORIDA

was too late, however, to altogether repair the injuries done to the army of the Southwest by the tardiness and default of the head of the War Department, which, as General Jackson said in an official report, threatened defeat and disaster to his command at New Orleans. Indignant public sentiment laid the blame of the capture of Washington, and of the humiliating disasters there, to the same negligence and default of this official, which led to his resignation soon after.

CHAPTER 2

General Jackson
Assumes Command

General Andrew Jackson had, in July, 1814, been appointed a major-general in the United States army, and assigned the command of the Southern department, with headquarters at Mobile. His daring and successful campaigns against the Indian allies of the British the year previous had won for him the confidence of the Government and of the people, and distinguished him as the man fitted for the emergency. At the beginning of the war British emissaries busily sought to enlist, arm, and equip all the Indians of the Southern tribes whom they could disaffect, as their allies, and to incite them to a war of massacre, pillage, and destruction against the white settlers, as they did with the savage tribes north of the Ohio River. In this they were successfully aided by Tecumseh, the Shawanee chief, and his brother, the Prophet. These were sons of a Creek mother and a Shawanee brave. By relationship, and by the rude eloquence of the former and the mystic arts and incantations of the latter, they brought into confederacy with Northern tribes—which they had organized as allies of the English in a last hope of destroying American power in the West—almost the entire Creek nation. These savages, though at peace under treaty and largely supported by the fostering aid of our Government, began hostilities after their usual methods of indiscriminate massacre and marauding destruction, regardless of age or sex or condition, against the exposed settlers. The latter sought refuge as they could in the rude stockade stations, but feebly garrisoned. At Fort Mims, on the Alabama River, nearly three hundred old men and women and children, with a small garrison of soldiers, were captured in a surprise attack by a large body of warriors, and all massacred in cold blood. This atrocious outbreak aroused the country, and led to speedy action for defence and terrible chastisement for the guilty perpetrators. The British officers offered rewards for scalps brought in, as under Proctor in the Northwest, and many scalps of men and women murdered were exchanged for this horrible blood-money.

In October, 1813, General Jackson led twenty-five hundred Tennessee militia, who had been speedily called out, into the Creek country in Alabama. A corps of one thousand men from Georgia, and another of several hundred from the territory of Mississippi, invaded the same from different directions. Sanguinary battles with the savages were fought by Jackson's command at Tallasehatche, Talladega, Hillabee, Autosse, Emuckfau, Tohopeka, and other places, with signal success to the American arms in every instance. The villages and towns of the enemy were burned, their fields and gardens laid waste, and the survivors driven to the woods and swamps. Not less than five thousand of the great Ocmulgee nation perished in this war, either in battle or from the ruinous results of their treachery after. Nearly one thousand of the border settlers were sacrificed, one half of whom were women and children or other non-combatants, the victims of the malignant designs and arts of British emissaries. The chief of the Creeks sued for peace, and terms were negotiated by General Jackson on the 14th of August, 1814.

From his headquarters at Mobile, in September, 1814, General Jackson, with sleepless vigilance, was anticipating and watching the movements of the British upon the Gulf coast, and marshalling his forces to resist any attack. There had been reported to him the arrival of a squadron of nine English ships in the harbour of Pensacola. Spain was at peace with our country, and it was due that the Spanish commandant of Florida, yet a province of Spain, should observe a strict neutrality pending hostilities. Instead of this comity of good faith and friendship, the Spanish officials had permitted this territory to become a refuge for the hostile Indians. Here they could safely treat with the British agents, from whom they received the implements of war, supplies of food and clothing, and the pay and emoluments incident to their services as allies in war. In violation of the obligations of neutrality, the Spanish officials not only tolerated this trespass on the territory of Florida, but, truckling to the formidable power and prestige of the great English nation, they dared openly to insult our own Government by giving aid and encouragement to our enemy in their very capital.

The most important and accessible point in Spanish Florida was Pensacola. Here the Governor, Gonzalez Maurequez, held court and dispensed authority over the province. The pride of the Spaniards in the old country and in Florida and Louisiana was deeply wounded over the summary sale of the territory of Louisiana by Napoleon to the United States in 1803; recalling the compulsory cession of the same to France by Spain in 1800. Naturally they resented with spirit what they deemed an indignity to the honour and sovereignty of their nation. The Spanish minister at Washington entered a solemn protest against the transaction; questions of boundaries soon after became a continuing cause of irritating dispute. The Dons contended that all east of the Mississippi River was Florida territory and subject to their jurisdiction. A military demonstration by General Wilkinson, then in command of the army of the Southwest, was ordered from Washington, opposition awed into silence, and the transfer made. In brief time after the boundaries of Florida were fixed on the thirty-first degree of north latitude, and east of a line near to the present boundary between Louisiana and Mississippi. Previously Mobile was the seat of government for Florida, but American aggression made the removal of the Government to Pensacola compulsory, and gave an additional cause of grievance to our sensitive neighbours. Under British auspices and promises of protection, the Governor displayed his resentment.

To confirm the report that came to him at Mobile of the arrival of an English squadron in Pensacola Bay, and of treacherous aid and comfort being given by the Spanish Governor, Jackson sent as spies some friendly Indians to the scene of operations, with instructions to furtively observe all that could be seen and known, and report to him the information. It was confirmed that the ships were in the harbour, and that a camp of English soldiers was in the town; that a considerable body of Indian recruits had been armed and were being drilled, and that runners had been dispatched to the country to invite and bring others to the coast to join them as comrades in arms. A few days after, a friendly courier brought news that several hundred marines had landed from the ships, that Colonel Nichols in command and his staff were guests of Governor Maurequez, and that the British flag was floating with the flag of Spain over one of the Spanish forts.

An order issued about this time by Colonel Nichols to his troops, followed by a proclamation to the people of Louisiana and Kentucky, revealed in visible outlines something of the purposes and plans of the menacing armaments. He advised his command that the troops would probably soon be called upon to endure long and tedious marches through forests and swamps in an enemy's country, and exhorted them to conciliate their Indian allies and "never to give them just cause of offense." He addressed the most inflammatory appeals to the national pride and prejudices of the French people of Louisiana, and to supposed discontented citizens of Kentucky, whose grievances had grown out of their neglect by the National Government or been engendered by the arts of designing politicians and adventurers.

CHAPTER 3

Battle at Mobile Bay

General Jackson strongly suspected that Louisiana would be invaded, and that New Orleans was designed to be the main and final point of attack. Yet he was led to believe that the British would attempt the capture of Mobile first, for strategic reasons. Early in September he reinforced the garrison of Fort Bowyer, situated thirty miles south of Mobile. This fortification, mounting twenty cannon, commanded the entrance to the harbour. It was garrisoned by one hundred and thirty men, under the command of Major William Lawrence. On the fifteenth of September the attack was made by a squadron of four ships of war, assisted by a land force of seven hundred marines and Indians. Though the enemy mounted ninety-two pieces of artillery, in the assault made they were defeated and driven off to sea again, with a loss of two hundred killed and wounded, the flagship of the commander sent to the bottom, and the remaining ships seriously damaged.

CHAPTER 4

Assault and Capture of Pensacola

Incensed at the open and continued violations of neutrality by the Spanish Governor, who had permitted Pensacola to be made a recruiting camp for the arming and drilling of their Indian allies by the British, General Jackson determined to march his army against this seat of government, and to enforce the observance of neutrality on the part of the Spanish commandant at the point of the bayonet if need be. He had removed his headquarters to Fort Montgomery, where by the first of November his command consisted of one thousand regular troops and two thousand militia, mainly from Tennessee and Mississippi—in all, about three thousand men. With these he set out for Pensacola, and on the evening of the sixth of November encamped within two miles of the town. He sent in Major Peire, bearing a flag of truce to the Governor, with a message that Pensacola must no longer be a refuge and camp for the enemies of the United States, and that the town must be surrendered, together with the forts. The messenger was fired on and driven back from Fort St. Michael, over which the British flag had been floating jointly with the flag of Spain. The firing was done by British troops harboured within. Governor Maurequez disavowed knowledge of the outrage, but refused to surrender his authority. The next morning the intrepid Jackson entered the town and carried by storm its defences, the British retreating to their ships and putting off to sea. Fort Barrancas was blown up by the enemy, to prevent the Americans from turning its guns upon the escaping British vessels. The Spanish commandant made profuse apologies, and pledged that he would in future observe a strict neutrality.

Jackson, fearing another attempt to capture Mobile by the retiring fleet, withdrew from Pensacola and marched for the former place, arriving there on the eleventh of November. At Mobile, messengers from those in highest authority at New Orleans met him, urging that he hasten there with his army and at once begin measures for the defence of that city. Information had been received by W.C. Claiborne, then Governor of Louisiana, from a highly credited source—most unexpected, but most fortunate and welcome—that the vast British armament of ships and men rendezvousing in the West Indies was about ready to sail, and that New Orleans was assuredly the objective point of the expedition.

Chapter 5

Lafitte, the Pirate of the Gulf

The informant was the celebrated Captain Jean Lafitte, the leader of the reputed pirates of the Gulf, who had been outlawed by an edict of our Government. The circumstances were so romantic, and displayed such a patriotic love for and loyalty to our country, that they are worthy of brief mention. As Byron wrote, he—

Left a corsair's name to other times,
Linked with one virtue and a thousand crimes.

But this does injustice to these *marauders of the sea*, who put in a plea of extenuation. The disparity of their virtues and their crimes is overwrought in the use of poetic license. Before the period of the conquest of Guadeloupe by the English, the French Government in force on that island had granted permits to numerous privateersmen to prey upon the commerce of the enemy, as our own Government had done in two wars. Now they could no longer enter the ports of that or of any other of the West India islands, with their prizes and cargoes. Lafitte and his daring sea-rovers made of the Bay of Barataria, on the Gulf coast sixty miles south of New Orleans, a place of rendezvous and head-quarters for their naval and commercial adventures. From this point they had ready and almost unobserved communication by navigable bayous with New Orleans and the marts beyond. They formed a sequestered colony on the shores of Barataria, and among the bold followers of Lafitte there were nearly one hundred men skilled in navigation, expert in the use of artillery, and familiar with every bay and inlet within one hundred miles of the Crescent City. Their services, if attainable, might be made invaluable in the invasion and investment of New Orleans contemplated by the British, who through their spies kept well informed of the conditions of the environment of the city. The time seemed opportune to win them over. If not pirates under our laws, they were smugglers who found it necessary to market the rich cargoes they captured and brought in as privateersmen. Barred out by other nations, New Orleans was almost the lone market for their wares and for their distribution inland. Many merchants and traders favoured this traffic, and had grown rich in doing so, despite the severity of our revenue laws against smuggling and the protests of other nations with whom we were friendly.

One of the Lafitte brothers and other leaders of the outlawed community were under arrest and held for trial in the Federal Court at New Orleans at this time. From Pensacola, Colonel Nichols sent Captains Lockyer, of the navy, and Williams, of the army, as emissaries to offer to the Baratarian outlaws the most enticing terms and the most liberal rewards, provided they would enlist in the service of the British in their invasion of Louisiana. Lafitte received them cautiously, but courteously. He listened to their overtures, and feigned deep interest in their mission. Having fully gained their confidence, they delivered to him sealed packages from Colonel Nichols himself, offering thirty thousand dollars in hand, high commissions in the English service for the officers, and liberal pay for the men, on condition that the Baratarians would ally themselves with the British forces. After the reading of these documents, the emissaries began to enlarge on the subject, insisting on the great advantages to result on enlisting in the service of his Britannic Majesty, and the opportunity afforded of acquiring fame and fortune. They were imprudent enough to disclose to Lafitte the purpose and plans of the great English flotilla in the waters of the Gulf, now ready to enter upon their execution. The army of invasion, supported by the navy of England, would be invincible, and all lower Louisiana would soon be in the possession of the British. They would then penetrate the upper country, and act in concert with the forces in Canada. On plausible pretexts the emissaries were delayed for a day or two, and then returned to their ship lying at anchor outside the pass into the harbour. Lafitte lost little time in visiting New Orleans and laying before Governor Claiborne the letters of Colonel Nichols and the sensational information he had received from the British envoys.

It was this intelligence which was borne in haste to General Jackson at Mobile, by the couriers mentioned previously. The Lafittes promptly tendered the services of themselves, their officers, and their men, in a body to the American army, and pledged to do all in their power, by sea and land, to defeat and repel the invading enemy, on condition that the Government would accept their enlistment, pardon them of all offenses, and remove from over them the ban of outlawry. This was all finally done, and no recruits of Jackson's army rendered more gallant and effective service, for their numbers, in the stirring campaign that followed. They outclassed the English gunners in artillery practice, and showed themselves to be veterans as marines or soldiers.

On receipt of this information of Lafitte, confirmed from other secret and reliable sources, the citizens were aroused. A mass-meeting was held in New Orleans and a Committee of Safety appointed, composed of Edward Livingston, Pierre Fouchet, De la Croix, Benjamin Morgan, Dominique Bouligny, J.A. Destrahan, John Blanque, and Augustine Macarte, who acted in concert with Governor Claiborne, and with the Legislature called into session.

CHAPTER 6

Jackson Arrives in New Orleans

General Jackson left Mobile on the twenty-first of November and arrived with his little army at New Orleans on the second of December, and established headquarters at 984 (now 406) Royal Street. He found the city well-nigh defenceless, while petty factions divided the councils of leaders and people, especially rife among the members of the Legislature. There was, incident to recent changes of sovereignties and conditions of nationalities, serious disaffection on the part of a most respectable element of the population of Louisiana and Florida toward the American Government. The French and Spaniards, who mainly composed the population, intensely loved their native countries with a patriotic pride. They knew allegiance to no other, until a few years before, by the arbitrary edicts of Napoleon, all of Louisiana was sold and transferred to the United States. Other causes of irritation added to the bitterness of resentment felt by the old Spanish element. Spain tenaciously insisted on enforcing her claims of sovereignty to all territory from the east bank of the Mississippi to the Perdido River, on the east line of Alabama. But the American settlers within the same became turbulent, and in October, 1810, these bold bordermen organized a filibustering force of some strength, captured and took possession of Baton

Rouge, killing Commandant Grandpre, who yet asserted there the authority of Spain. When Congress met, in December, 1810, an act was passed in secret session authorizing the President to take military possession of the disputed coast country in certain contingencies. Under orders from Washington, General Wilkinson, with a force of six hundred regulars, marched against Mobile, took possession of the Spanish fort, Charlotte, and caused the garrison to withdraw to Pensacola.

This precipitate action—the British envoy protesting against such informal occupation—was justified at home on the plea of strong grounds of suspicion that England herself might suddenly assert sovereignty over the same territory under secret treaty with Spain. Amid these rude and revolutionary proceedings, all within a decade of years, necessarily there followed a tumult of differing sentiment and contentions among the Spanish, French, and American people of the section. Fortunately the French element were of a nativity whose country had been for generations the inveterate enemy of the English, our common foe. If there were any who felt resentment before over the enforced change of allegiance from beloved France to the stranger sovereignty, when the crisis of campaign and battle came none were more gallant and brave in meeting the invading enemy.

On the ninth of December the great English flotilla appeared off Chandeleur Islands, and came to anchor near to Ship Island, the shallowness of the water not permitting the nearer approach to the main shore of vessels so large. The British authorities yet believed that the destination of this fleet was unknown to the Americans ashore; but in this they were mistaken, as they afterward admitted. The inadequacy of men and means and measures to properly meet and repel such an invading force, as mentioned before, was mainly due to the tardy negligence of the department at

POSITIONS OF THE
AMERICAN & BRITISH ARMIES
NEAR NEW ORLEANS
JANY. 8TH. 1815

Washington. The sleepless vigilance and untiring energy of General Jackson was in marked contrast to this, not only within his own military jurisdiction, but in the whole region around. His trusty spies, pale and dusky, were everywhere, and little escaped his attention. The situation was now critical in the extreme. Fortunately, the unbounded confidence all had in their military chief inspired hope and infused energy among the people. He had never been defeated in battle. If any one could wrest victory now out of the inauspicious and chaotic conditions that threatened disaster, they believed it to be General Jackson.

Marvellous was the change wrought by his timely appearance on the theatre of active operations. The partial attempts to adopt measures of defence were of little avail. The joint committee of the Legislature to act in concert with Governor Claiborne, Commodore Patterson, and the military commandant, had done but little as yet. There was wanting the concentration of power always needed in military operations. Latour, in his "Memoirs of the War of 1814-15," graphically describes the condition of affairs as he saw and knew them to exist:

Confidence was wanting in the civil and military authorities, and a feeling of distrust and gloomy apprehension pervaded the minds of the citizens. Petty disputes on account of two committees of defence, unfortunately countenanced by the presence and influence of several public officials, had driven the people to despondency. They complained, not without cause, that the Legislature wasted time, and consumed the money of the State, in idle discussions, when both time and money should have been devoted to measures of defence. The banks had suspended payment of their notes, and credit was gone. The moneyed men had drawn in their funds, and loaned their money at the ruinous rates of three or four per cent per month. The situation seemed desperate; in case of attack, none could hope to be saved only by miracle, or by the wisdom and genius of a great commander.

After his habit of giving his personal attention to every detail, General Jackson, on his arrival, visited Fort St. Philip, ordered the wooden barracks removed, and had mounted additional heavy artillery. He caused two more batteries to be constructed, one on the opposite bank of the Mississippi, and the other half a mile above, with twenty-four pounders in position, thus fully guarding the approach by the mouth of the river. He then proceeded to Chef Menteur, as far as Bayou Sauvage, and ordered a battery erected at that point. He continued to fortify or obstruct the larger bayous whose waters gave convenient access to the city between the Mississippi and the Gulf.

As early as July before, the Secretary of War, in view of the formidable armaments of England, had made requisition of the several States for ninety-three thousand five hundred men for general defensive purposes, under a law of Congress enacted the previous April. The quota of Kentucky was fifty-five hundred infantry; of Tennessee, twenty-five hundred infantry; of Mississippi territory, five hundred infantry, and of Louisiana, one thousand infantry. That portion of the quota of Kentucky destined for New Orleans, twenty-two hundred men, and a portion of the quota of Tennessee, embarked upon flatboats to float fifteen hundred miles down the Ohio and Mississippi waters, had not arrived on the tenth of December. Through the energetic efforts of the Governor, aided by Major Edward Livingston and the Committee of Safety, the quota of Louisiana was made up. With these, General Coffee's Tennesseans, Major Hinds' Mississippians, and one thousand regular troops, there were less than three thousand men for defensive operations yet available.

Chapter 7

Gunboats & Barges

An event was soon to happen which seemed for the time an irreparable disaster to the American cause. Commodore Daniel T. Patterson, in command of the American naval forces, on learning of the approach of the British fleet, sent Lieutenant Thomas ap Catesby Jones, with five gunboats, one tender, and a dispatch boat toward the passes out to Ship Island, to watch the movements of the British vessels. This little flotilla, barely enough for scout duty at sea, was the extent of our naval forces in the Gulf waters near. The orders were to fall back, if necessary, from near Cat Island to the Rigolets; and there, if hard pressed, to sink or be sunk by the enemy. Moving in waters too shallow for the large English ships to pursue, until the thirteenth, Lieutenant Jones sailed for Bay St. Louis. Sighting a large number of the enemy's barges steering for Pass Christian, he headed for the Rigolets. But the wind having died away and an adverse current set in, the little fleet could get no farther than the channel inside of Melheureux Island, being there partially grounded. Early on the morning of the fourteenth, a flotilla of barges formed in line was discovered coming from the direction of the enemy's ships, evidently to overtake and attack the becalmed gunboats. The two tenders, lying beyond the aid of the latter, were captured after a spirited resistance. The guns of these were now turned upon Lieutenant Jones' gunboats in a combined attack of the fleet of barges, forty-five in number, and a supporting squad of marines. The total equipment was twelve hundred men and forty-five pieces of artillery. The American defensive forces were seven small gunboats, manned by thirty guns and one hundred and eighty men. The enemy's oarsmen advanced their entire fleet in line of battle until the fire from the gunboats caused severe losses and some confusion in the movements of the barges. They then separated in three divisions and renewed the attack. The battle became general, and was contested fiercely for nearly two hours, when the gunboats, overpowered by numbers, were forced to surrender, losing six men killed and thirty-five wounded, among the latter Lieutenants Jones, Speddin, and McKeever, each in command of a boat. Several barges of the enemy were sunk, while their losses in killed and wounded were estimated at two to three hundred. Among the wounded were Captain Lockyer, in command, and other officers.

The preparations for defence on shore were now pushed forward with redoubled energy. General Jackson gave unremitting attention to the fortifying of all points which seemed available for the approach of the enemy; it was impossible to know at what point he might choose to make his first appearance on land. Captain Newman, in command of Fort Petit Coquille, at the Rigolets, next to Lake Pontchartrain, was reinforced, and the order given to defend the post to the last extremity. If compelled to abandon it, he was instructed to fall back on Chef Menteur. Swift messengers were sent to Generals Carroll and Thomas to make all speed possible with the Tennessee and Kentucky troops on their way to New Orleans. Also, a courier was dispatched to General Winchester, commanding at Mobile, warning of the possible danger of another attack on that place, since the loss of the gunboats. Major Lacoste, with the dragoons of Feliciana and his militia battalion of coloured men, was directed, with two pieces of artillery, to take post at the confluence of Bayous Sauvage and Chef Menteur, throw up a redoubt, and guard the road. Major Plauche was sent with his battalion to Bayou St. John, north of the city, Major Hughes being in command of Fort St. John. Captain Jugeant was instructed to enlist and form into companies all the Choctaw Indians he could collect, a mission that proved nearly barren of results. The Baratarians, mustered into ranks and drilled for important services under their own officers, Captains Dominique You, Beluche, Sougis, Lagand, and Golson, were divided out to the forts named, and to other places where expert gunners were most needed.

On the eighteenth of December a grand review of the Louisiana troops was held by Jackson in front of the old Cathedral, now Jackson Square. The day was memorable by many incidents, not all in harmony with the purposes and plans of the civil and military leaders of defence. The entire population of the city and vicinity were present to witness the novel scenes, men and women vying with each other in applauding and enthusing the martial ardour of the soldiers on parade. Such an army, hastily improvised in a few brief days from city, country, and towns, made up of a composite of divergent race elements, as was that of the Louisiana contingent with the command of Jackson at New Orleans, was perhaps never paralleled in the history of warfare before. Major Plauche's battalion of uniformed companies was made up mainly of French and Spanish Creoles, with some of American blood, enlisted from the city; and from the same source came Captain Beale's Rifle Company, mostly American residents. The Louisiana militia, under General Morgan, were of the best element of the country parishes, of much the same race-types as Plauche's men, of newer material, and without uniforms. Then came the battalion of Louisiana free men of colour, nearly three hundred strong, led by Major Lacoste, and another battalion of men of colour, two hundred and fifty in number, commanded by Major Daquin, recruited from the refugees in New Orleans from St. Domingo, who had taken part in the bloody strifes in that island, and who bore like traditional hatred to the English, with all who spoke the French tongue. Add to the above a small detachment of Choctaw Indians; and lastly, the loyal pirates of Lafitte, who were patriotic enough to scorn the gold of England, and brave enough to offer their services and their lives, if need be, to the cause of our country; and together, these give us a picture of the men under review, whom Jackson was to lead to battle in a few days against the best-trained troops of Europe. Though of new material, and suddenly called into service, this provincial contingent of twelve hundred men, animated with the spirit of battle against an invading foe, proved themselves, when ably officered, the equals of the best troops in the field.

CHAPTER 8

Martial Law

On the sixteenth, two days before the review, General
Jackson issued from his headquarters an order declaring
"the city and environs of New Orleans under martial law."
This imperious edict was resorted to in the firm belief that
only the exercise of supreme military authority could awe
into silence all opposition to defensive operations. Every
person entering the city was required to report himself to
headquarters, and any one departing from it must procure
a pass. The street lamps were extinguished at nine o'clock
at night, and every one found passing after that hour was
subject to arrest. All persons capable of bearing arms who
did not volunteer were pressed into the military or naval
service. Rumours were rife that British spies were secretly
prowling in the city, and coming into the American camp.
Reports of disloyal utterances and suspicious proceedings
on the part of certain citizens came repeatedly to the ears of
the commander-in-chief. More serious yet, he was aroused
to fierce anger by personal and direct intelligence that certain leading and influential members of the Legislature favoured a formal capitulation and surrender of Louisiana to
the enemy, by that body, in the event of a formidable invasion, for the greater security of their persons and property.
These persons had circulated a story that Jackson would

burn the city and all valuable property in reach rather than let it fall into the hands of the British.

Determined that disloyalty should find no foothold to mar his military plans, or to disaffect the soldiery or citizens, General Jackson, on the day previous to his declaration of martial law, issued the following spirited order:

To the Citizens of New Orleans

The Major-General commanding, has, with astonishment and regret, learned that great consternation and alarm pervade your city. It is true the enemy is on our coast and threatens to invade our territory; but it is equally true that, with union, energy, and the approbation of Heaven, we will beat him at every point his temerity may induce him to set foot on our soil. The General, with still greater astonishment, has heard that British emissaries have been permitted to propagate seditious reports among you, that the threatened invasion is with a view to restore the country to Spain, from the supposition that some of you would be willing to return to your ancient government. Believe not such incredible tales; your Government is at peace with Spain. It is the vital enemy of your country,—the common enemy of mankind, the highway robber of the world, that threatens you. He has sent his hirelings among you with this false report, to put you off your guard, that you may fall an easy prey. Then look to your liberties, your property, the chastity of your wives and daughters. Take a retrospect of the conduct of the British army at Hampton, and other places where it entered our country, and every bosom which glows with patriotism and virtue, will be inspired with indignation, and pant for the arrival of the hour when we shall meet and revenge these outrages against the laws of civilization and humanity.

The General calls upon the inhabitants of the city to trace this unfounded report to its source, and bring the propagator to condign punishment. The rules and articles of war annex the punishment of death to any person holding secret correspondence with the enemy, creating false alarm, or supplying him with provision. The General announces his determination rigidly to execute the martial law in all cases which may come within his province.

By command.

Thomas L. Butler

Aid-de-camp

CHAPTER 8

Bayou Bienvenue and
the British Spies

Bayou Bienvenue, formerly called St. Frances River, drains all the waters of a swamp-basin, of triangular form and about eighty square miles in surface, bounded on the west by New Orleans, on the northwest by Chef Menteur, and on the east by Lake Borgne, into which it empties. It receives the waters of several other bayous from the surrounding cypress swamps and prairies. It is navigable for vessels of one hundred tons burden as far as the junction with old Piernas Canal, twelve miles from its mouth. It is about one hundred and twenty yards in width, and has from six to nine feet of water at the bar, according to the flow of the tides. Its principal branch is Bayou Mazant, which runs to the southwest and receives the waters of the canals of the old plantations of Villere, Lacoste, and Laronde, on and near which the British army encamped, about eight miles below New Orleans. The banks of these bayous, which drain the swamp lands on either side of the Mississippi, are usually about twelve feet below the banks of the river, which have been elevated by the deposit of sediment from overflows for centuries. These slopes, from the banks back to the swamps, usually ten to eighteen hundred yards, drain off the waters and form the tillable lands of the sugar and cotton planters.

They are protected from overflows by levees thrown up on the banks of the river. These plantation lands formed the only ground in this country for the encampment of a large army, or available for a march on New Orleans. On nearly all the large sugar plantations canals were cut from the bank of the river running back to the swamp, to furnish at high tides water-power for mills which did the grinding or sawing for the plantations.

Bayous Bienvenue and Mazant, as mentioned, formed a waterway from Lake Borgne to the rear of the plantations of Villere, Lacoste, and Laronde, situated but two or three hours' easy march to the city, to which there was a continuous roadway through the plantation lands between the river and the swamps. The enemy was fully informed of every point of approach by spies within the military lines, and since the capture of the gunboats determined on an attempt to secretly invade the environing country, and to assault and capture New Orleans by surprise. But one mile from Lake Borgne, on the low bank of Bayou Bienvenue, was a village of Spanish and Portuguese fishermen and their families. From the bayous and adjacent lakes they furnished the city markets with fish, and were familiar with every body of water and every nook and inlet for many miles around. A number of these became notorious as spies in the pay of the British. Of this treacherous little colony, the names of Maringuier, Old Luiz, Francisco, Graviella, Antonio el Italiano, El Campechano, Mannellilo, and Garcia became known as connected with this disloyalty. These served the English as pilots to their barges, as guides to the best approaches to New Orleans, and as ready spies within and without. The English commander in charge sent Captain Peddie, of the army, on the twentieth of December, as a spy in the disguise of one of these fishermen, to inspect and report upon the feasibility of entering with the army at the mouth of Bayou Bienvenue, landing at the plantations above and marching suddenly by this route on the city. Old Luiz and two others of the fishermen were his guides. He safely and without suspicion penetrated to Villere's plantation, viewed the field for encampment there, and noted the easy route of approach to the city, without an obstruction in the way. His report being most favourable, the British officer in command decided at once on invasion and attack from this direction.

CHAPTER 9

The British Land Near Villere's Plantation

By Jackson's order, Major Villere, son of General Villere, the owner of the plantation, placed a picket of twelve men at Fisherman's Village on the twenty-first, to watch and report promptly in case the enemy appeared there. After midnight, near the morning of the twenty-third, five advance barges bearing British troops glided noiselessly into Bienvenue from Lake Borgne, capturing the picket of twelve men without firing a gun. Soon after, the first division of the invading army, twenty-five hundred strong, under command of Colonel Thornton, appeared in eighty barges, and passed up the bayous to Villere's canal, where a landing was effected by the dawn of day. After a brief rest and breakfast, the march of two miles was made to Villere's plantation, arriving there at half-past eleven. The troops at once surrounded the house of General Villere, and surprised and made prisoners a company of the Third Louisiana Militia stationed there. Major Villere, after capture, escaped through a window at the risk of his life, reached the river bank and crossed over in a small boat, and hastened to New Orleans with the startling news. Colonel Laronde also escaped, and reached headquarters in the early afternoon; on the day before he had reported the sighting of several suspicious vessels out upon Lake Borgne, seemingly to reconnoitre.

Jackson had ordered Majors Latour and Tatum, of his engineer corps, to reconnoitre in the direction of the Laronde and Lacoste plantations, and to carefully examine this avenue of approach by the enemy. These officers left the city at eleven o'clock, and had reached Laronde's, when they met several persons fleeing toward the city, who told them of the arrival of the British at Villere's, and of the capture of the outpost there. It was then but half-past one o'clock. The two scouts put spurs to their horses, and by two o'clock the General was informed of the facts. With that heroic promptness and intuition characteristic and ever present with him, he exclaimed with fierce emphasis: "By the eternal! the enemy shall not sleep upon our soil!" The invading movement was a complete surprise, and there was not yet a defensive work to obstruct the march of the British upon the coveted city. Only genius and courage of the highest order could have met successfully such an emergency, and Jackson alone seemed equal to the occasion.

CHAPTER 10

Night–Battle—23rd of December

Orders were issued rapidly, as the report of the alarm-gun gave notice to all to be ready. The troops were stationed within a radius of a few miles of the city, in garrisons. Major Plauche was summoned to bring down his battalion of uniformed volunteers from Bayou St. John, which summons was obeyed in a run all the way. General Coffee, encamped four miles above the city, under similar order, was at headquarters within one hour. Colonel McRae, with the Seventh regulars, Lieutenant Spotts, with two pieces of artillery, and Lieutenant Bellevue, with a detachment of marines, were all formed on the road near Montruil's plantation. Coffee's riflemen and Hinds' Mississippi dragoons formed the advance in the order of march. Beale's Orleans Rifles followed closely after, and by four o'clock these had taken position at Rodrique's Canal. The battalion of men of colour, under Major Daquin, the Forty-fourth regulars, under Captain Baker, and Plauche's men, were in close supporting distance.

Commodore Patterson was requested to arm such vessels lying in the river as were ready, and to drop down and take station opposite the enemy. The schooner *Carolina* was put in position; the sloop of war *Louisiana* could not steer in the stream. Governor Claiborne, with the First, Second, and Fourth Louisiana Militia, occupied a post in the plain of Gentilly, to cover the city on the side of Chef Menteur. A picket of five mounted men was fired on near the line of Laronde's and Lacoste's plantations, and driven in about four o'clock. A negro was apprehended, who had been sent by the British with printed copies of a proclamation in Spanish and French, in terms as follows: "Louisianians! remain quiet in your houses; your slaves shall be preserved to you, and your property respected. We make war only against Americans." This was signed by Admiral Cochrane and General Keene. Other copies were found.

About nightfall the troops were formed in line of battle, the left composed of a part of Coffee's men, Beale's Rifles, the Mississippi dragoons, and some other mounted riflemen, in all about seven hundred and thirty men, General Coffee in command, Colonel Laronde as guide. Under cover of the darkness, they took position back of the plantation of the latter. The right formed on a perpendicular line from the river to the garden of Laronde's plantation, and on its principal avenue. The artillery occupied the high road, supported by a detachment of marines. On the left of the artillery were stationed the Seventh and Forty-fourth regulars, Plauche's and Daquin's battalions, and a squad of Choctaw Indians, all under the command of Colonel Ross.

The second invading division of the British army, made up of the Twenty-first, Forty-fourth, and Ninety-third Regiments, with a corps of artillery, in all about twenty-five hundred men, was disembarked at the terminus of Villere Canal at half-past seven o'clock in the evening of the twenty-third, just as the roar of the ship's cannon announced the opening of the night battle. At seven o'clock Commodore Patterson had anchored the Carolina in the Mississippi, as requested, in front of the British camp, and but a good musket-shot away. Such was the security felt by the enemy in camp that they stood upon the levee and viewed her as a common boat plying the river. Within thirty minutes she opened upon the enemy a destructive fire which spread consternation and havoc throughout their camp. In half an hour more they were driven out, with many killed and wounded. About eight o'clock the troops on the right, led by Jackson himself, began the attack on the enemy's left. The Seventh and Forty-fourth regulars became hotly engaged along the line, supported by McRae's artillery. Plauche's and Daquin's battalions coming up, the fighting became furious from the road to Laronde's garden. The British were forced back within the limits of Lacoste's plantation, the combatants being often intermingled and fighting hand-to-hand, almost undistinguishable in the darkness of night, made denser by the smoke of battle and the gathering fog.

Meanwhile, Coffee's troops, from the rear of Laronde's plantation, were moved to the boundary limits of Lacoste and Villere, with a view of taking the enemy in the rear. Coffee extended his front and ordered his men to move forward in silence and to fire without orders, taking aim as best they could. They drove the enemy before them, and took a second position in front of Lacoste's plantation. Here was posted the Eighty-fifth Regiment of the British army, which was forced back by the first fire toward their main camp. Captain Beale's Riflemen advanced on the left into the British camp at Villere's, driving the enemy before them and taking some prisoners, but sustained some loss before joining Coffee again. Coffee's division finally took a last position in front of the old levee, near Laronde's boundary, where it harassed the enemy as they fell back, driven by Jackson on the right. By ten o'clock the British had fallen back to their camp in discomfiture, where they were permitted to lay in comparative quiet until morning, except their harassment from the artillery fire of the schooner Carolina. In the darkness and confusion of combat at dead of night lines were broken and order lost at times, until it was difficult to distinguish friends from foes. General Jackson led his troops back to the opening point of the attack and rested them there until morning, when he fell back over one mile to Rodrique's Canal, the position selected for the defence of the city.

Three hundred and fifty of the Louisiana militia, under command of General David Morgan, were stationed at English Turn, seven miles below Villere's, and nearly fourteen miles from New Orleans. Intelligence of the arrival of the British at Villere's, on the twenty-third, reached General Morgan's camp at one o'clock in the afternoon of the day. Officers and men expressed an eagerness to be led against the enemy; but General Morgan, not having then received orders from Jackson to that effect, deemed it prudent to hold them waiting in camp. At half-past seven o'clock, when the guns from the *Carolina* were heard bringing on the battle, it was found difficult to restrain them longer. Morgan finally, at the urgent request of his officers, gave orders to go forward, which the troops received with ardour. They reached a point near Jumonville's plantation, just below Villere's, when a picket guard in advance met a picket force of the enemy and fired on it; the fire was returned. A reconnoitre failing to discover the numbers and position of the enemy in his front, Morgan took a position in a field until three o'clock in the morning, when he marched his men back to camp. The failure of this command to join issue in this battle, in concert with the other commands of Jackson's army, was apparently most unfortunate. The records do not show what orders, if any, were sent from headquarters by Jackson to General Morgan in summoning his forces in the afternoon of the day for the attack at night.

It is barely possible that the General neglected to dispatch an order to, or to communicate with, the commander of so important a body of troops, in numbers nearly one fifth of the entire American forces engaged, in a critical hour when every available soldier was needed on the field of combat. A swift messenger sent by Jackson from headquarters at two o'clock, as to other outpost commands, could easily have reached English Turn at five o'clock. General Morgan knew that the invading army were in bivouac seven miles above. By eight o'clock he could have had his troops in attacking distance of the enemy, and in their rear. When Jackson and Coffee assaulted the British lines at eight o'clock, and drove them back in confusion upon their camp, a spirited surprise attack by Morgan's command in the rear, any moment before nine o'clock, would probably have routed the entire British division engaged and forced them to lay down their arms or retreat to their boats. He did move his command forward, and halt them at some distance from the enemy, but it was probably too late. The battle was over and the opportunity gone.

An after-incident throws a ray of light upon the criticism of the day upon the above affair. Honourable Magloire Guichard, President of the House of Representatives, in his testimony before the Committee of Inquiry on the military measures employed by Jackson against the Legislature, said:

On the twenty-seventh of December, when I got home, I found Colonel Declouet (of Morgan's command), who had just crossed the river. Amid the conversation of the evening, I expressed my surprise at his not having attacked the British from the lower side, on the night of the twenty-third; that had he done so with the men under his command, at the same time with the troops coming from the city, all would have

58

terminated on that evening, and the British would have laid down their arms. He expressed great sorrow that he had not been the master to do so. He declared that this was his intention, but that General Morgan refused to comply with his request. Afterwards, having resolved to come toward midnight to reconnoitre, they had met with a small picket, who fired upon them; they returned the fire, and then retired.

The British loss in this initial night-battle is put by our authorities at four to five hundred in killed, wounded, and prisoners. Their own official reports admit three to five hundred. The Americans had twenty-four killed, one hundred and fifteen wounded, and seventy-four made prisoners. The fall of Colonel Lauderdale, of Mississippi, was much lamented.

So unique in the annals of military experience was this fiercely fought night-battle, so startling in its surprise of the bold and confident Britons, and so characteristic of Jackson's grim humour of war, that it is interesting to know the impressions it made upon the minds of the enemy. With this view, we quote a vivid description from the history of an English officer who was in the campaigns against Napoleon, with Ross and Pakenham in America, and who was a participant in this battle, Captain Robert Gleig. He says:

> About half-past seven at night our attention was drawn to a large vessel which seemed to be stealing up the river, opposite our camp, when her anchor was dropped and her sails quietly furled. She was repeatedly hailed, but gave no answer. An alarm spread through our bivouac, and all thought of sleep was abandoned. Several musket shots were fired at her, when we heard a commanding voice cry out: "Give them this for the honour of America!" The words were instantly fol-

lowed by the flashes of her guns, and a deadly shower of grape swept down numbers in our camp.

Against this dreadful fire we had nothing as yet to oppose. We sought shelter under the levee, and listened in painful silence to the pattering of shot which fell among our troops, and to the shrieks and groans of the wounded who lay near by. The night was dark as pitch. Except the flashes of the enemy's guns, and the glare of our own deserted fires, not an object could be distinguished. In this state we lay helpless for nearly an hour, when a straggling fire of musketry, driving in our pickets, warned us to prepare for a closer and more desperate strife. This fire was presently succeeded by a fearful yell, while the heavens became illuminated on all sides by a semi-circular blaze of musketry.

Rushing from under the bank, the Eighty-fifth and Ninety-fifth Regiments flew to support the pickets; while the Fourth, stealing to the rear, formed close column as a reserve. But to describe this action is out of the question, for it was such a battle as the annals of warfare can hardly parallel. Each officer, as he was able to collect twenty or thirty men around him, advanced into the midst of the enemy, where they fought hand to hand, bayonet to bayonet, and sword to sword, with the tumult and ferocity of Homer's combats before the walls of Troy. Attacked unexpectedly in the dark, and surrounded by enemies before we could arrange to oppose them, no order or discipline of war could be preserved. We were mingled with the Americans before we could tell whether they were friends or foes. The consequence was that more feats of individual gallantry were performed in the course of the conflict than many campaigns might have afforded. The combat having begun at eight in the evening, and long and obstinately contested, continued until three in the morning; but the victory was decidedly ours, for the Americans retreated in the greatest disorder, leaving us in possession of the field. Our losses, however, were enormous. Not less than five hundred men had fallen, many of whom were our first and best officers.

The recall being sounded, our troops were soon brought together, forming in front of the ground where we had at first encamped. Here we remained until the morn, when, to avoid the fire of the vessel, we betook ourselves to the levee on the bank, and lay down. Here we lay for some hours, worn out with fatigue and loss of sleep, and shivering in the cold of a frosty morning, not daring to light a fire or cook a meal. Whenever an attempt was made, the ship's guns opened on us. Thus was our army kept prisoners for an entire day.

This was not a field victory for either combatant, but rather a drawn battle, as each party fell back to the lines occupied at the opening. It was a very great victory for the Americans in its bearings on the final issues of the campaign. The attack of Jackson was to the British like a bolt of lightning from a clear sky. It paralyzed and checked them on the first day, and at the first place of their encampment on shore, and enabled him to adopt measures to beat back the invaders in every attempt they made for a further advance inland. The enemy had found an open way and expected an easy march, with a certainty that the Crescent City, by Christmas Day, would become an easy prey for their "Loot and Lust," as Admiral Cochrane is said to have promised. Instead of a garden of delights, they had walked into a death-trap at the gate of entrance. Confidence and prestige were shaken in the front of a foe equal in valour and as skilled in arms as themselves. The rude reception given by Jackson had compelled the army of the invaders to halt in its first camp, and to re-form, to reinforce, and to rehabilitate its plans, before daring another step forward. This delay, fatal to the British, probably saved the city. On the next morning early (of the twenty-fourth) the first division of the British army would have been reinforced by the second division landed on the night of the battle, giving five thousand fresh veteran troops in bivouac at Villere's, with which to march upon the city. It was but seven miles distant, with a broad, level highway leading to it. Jackson could have opposed to this army not over two thousand men in the open field, where every advantage would have been with the enemy. With the bravery and discipline the latter showed in the surprise-battle at night, they would have made an irresistible march to victory against the city, had not the invincible Jackson paralyzed them with this first blow. It was a master-stroke, worthy the genius of a great commander.

The valour of the English soldiers was rarely, if ever, surpassed on a bloody field of contest. There was no panic, no rout, no cowering under the murderous fire of the ship's guns, or when the blaze of musketry encircled them in the darkness of the night. Although the ranks were broken and little order prevailed, the men rallied to the calls of the nearest officers, and plunged into the thickest of the strife. Only this veteran discipline and stubborn British courage saved the enemy from rout and worse disaster. Colonel Thornton, the bravest and most skilful of the officers of the English army, as he repeatedly proved himself, commanded on this occasion. General Keene had not yet come up.

The American forces engaged were: United States regulars, Seventh Regiment, Major Peire, four hundred and sixty-five men, and Forty-fourth Regiment, Captain Baker, three hundred and thirty-one men; marines, Lieutenant Bellevue, sixty-six; artillery, McRae, twenty-two; Major Plauche's battalion, two hundred and eighty-seven; Major Daquin's battalion of St. Domingo men of colour, two hundred and ten; Choctaws, Captain Jugeant, eighteen; Coffee's Tennessee Brigade, five hundred and sixty-three; Orleans Rifles, Captain Beale, sixty-two; and Mississippi Dragoons, Major Hinds, one hundred and seven; in all, twenty-one hundred and thirty-one men.

CHAPTER 11
Jackson at Rodrique's Old Canal

As mentioned, Jackson occupied the line of Rodrique's Canal, two miles above the British camp at Villere's, and five miles below the city. The space from the river here back to the swamp was but seventeen hundred yards, making it an admirable line for defence. Early on the twenty-fourth every available man was put to work throwing up a breastwork on the upper side of the canal, while pieces of artillery were planted at commanding points for immediate emergency. Negroes from the adjacent plantations were called in to expedite the work of building the entrenchment and suitable redoubts, as had been done at other works of fortification and defence. On the twenty-fifth, General Morgan was ordered to abandon the post at English Turn and to move his command of Louisiana militia to a position on the right bank of the river, at Flood's plantation, opposite Jackson's camp.

CHAPTER 12

The Ship *Carolina* Burned

The enemy determined to destroy the ship *Carolina*, as she lay out in the river, from whose deadly broadsides by day and by night they had been so terribly harassed since the opening of the night battle of the twenty-third. Having brought up their artillery from their landing-place, they erected a battery commanding that part of the river, with a furnace for heating shot. On the twenty-seventh, they opened fire in range, and in fifteen minutes the schooner was set on fire by the red-hot missiles and burned to the water's edge. The fire of the battery was next directed against the *Louisiana*, a larger war-vessel, the preservation of which was of great importance. Lieutenant Thompson, in command, with the combined efforts of one hundred men of his crew, succeeded under fire of the battery in towing her beyond the range of the guns of the enemy.

On the evening of the twenty-seventh the British moved forward in force, drove in the American advance lines, and occupied Chalmette's plantation, one mile above Laronde's. During the night they began to establish several batteries along the river. At dawn of day on the twenty-eighth they advanced in columns on the road, preceded by several pieces of artillery, some playing upon the *Louisiana* and others on the American lines. The ship's crew waited until the columns of the enemy were well in range, when they opened upon them a destructive fire, which silenced their guns. While this oblique fire fell upon the flank of the British, the batteries on the American line answered them from the front with much effect. One shot from the *Louisiana* killed fifteen of the enemy's men. Some of his guns were dismounted, and he was driven from several of his batteries. In seven hours' cannonading the ship fired eight hundred shot. The enemy threw into the American ranks many Congreve rockets, evidently misled in the hope that these ugly-looking missiles would strike terror to the ranks of our troops. These soon learned that they were not so dangerous as they appeared. The infantry this day did not engage in more than heavy picket skirmishing, and in checking the demonstrations of the enemy on our lines. This movement all along the line was evidently a feint in force, to draw from Jackson's army information as to the powers of resistance it might offer and to ascertain its most vulnerable point of attack. The loss of the British this day was estimated at two hundred; that of the Americans much less, as they were mainly sheltered from the enemy's fire. There were nine killed and eight wounded.

CHAPTER 13

Defences on the
West Bank of the River

Realizing that the enemy might suddenly throw a force across the river, and by a flank movement up the right bank gain a position opposite the city, from which, by shot and shell, he might compel a surrender, Jackson sent Major Latour, chief of his engineer corps, to the west side, with orders to select a position most suitable for a fortified line in the rear of General Morgan's camp. Bois-Gervais Canal, three miles below New Orleans, was fixed upon, and one hundred and fifty negroes from the plantations near at once set to work. In six days they completed the parapet, with a glacis on the opposite side.

Commodore Patterson removed from the Louisiana a number of her guns, which he placed in battery in front of Jordon's plantation, on the right bank, with which he did important service to the end of the campaign. This formidable battery was formed to give a deadly flanking fire on the enemy's ranks from the opposite bank of the river. It was manned and served by sailors, mostly landed from the *Carolina* when she was burned. They had been enlisted about the city after the gunboats were destroyed; men of all nations, not a third of them speaking the English language. The constant daily fire of this battery caused the British to fall back from Chalmette's and Bienvenue's houses and to seek safer quarters in the rear, after the artillery duels of the twenty-eighth.

Captain Henly, of the late ship *Carolina*, was placed in command of a strong redoubt on the bank of the river, opposite New Orleans, around which was a fosse twenty-five feet in width, the earth from which was thrown up to form a steep glacis, from the summit of the wall serving as a parapet to the brink of the fosse. Here a battery of two twenty-four pounders commanded at once the road and the river back to the swamp.

The Tennesseans, placed on the left, and operating in the undergrowth of the woods of the swamp, were a continual terror to the British sentinels and outposts. Clad in their brown hunting-dress, they were indistinguishable in the bush, while with their long rifles they picked off some of the British daily. The entrenchment line was being daily strengthened.

CHAPTER 14

Great Artillery Duel—
1st of January

On the evening of the twenty-fifth, Sir Edward Pakenham arrived at the British headquarters, and at once as-
sumed chief command of the army in person. He was a
favourite of Lord Wellington in the Peninsular campaigns,
and held in high esteem by the English Government and
people. His presence imparted great enthusiasm to the officers and men of the army, a majority of whom had served
under him in other wars. The invading British forces were
now swelled to over ten thousand men for present service.
On the thirtieth and thirty-first, the enemy was ominously
busy in throwing up redoubts and in pushing his offensive
works in threatening nearness to our lines. In front of Bienvenue's house he constructed a battery, of hogsheads of
sugar taken from the near plantations, the season for grinding the cane and converting the product into sugar having
just closed. A redoubt was also begun at a point nearer the
wood, fronting the American left, and some guns mounted
by the thirty-first. A heavy cannonading was opened on this
day, from this and other batteries along the British front, to
which our own guns responded, including those of the marine battery across the river, until two in the afternoon.

Battle of New Orleans, January 8, 1815

These demonstrative movements of the enemy, with his busy reconnoitring, foreboded an attack in force.

In the night of the thirty-first he erected, under cover of darkness, two other batteries of heavy guns at a distance of six hundred yards from the front of Jackson's entrenchments, on a ditch running along the side of Chalmette's plantation, at distances of three and six hundred yards from the river. During the night the men working on the platforms and mounting the ordnance could be distinctly heard.

On the morning of the 1st of January, 1815, the earth was veiled by a dense fog until eight o'clock. As the misty cloud lifted above the horizon, the enemy opened up a terrific fire from his three batteries in front, mounting respectively two, eight, and eight pieces of heavy cannon. A meteor-like shower of Congreve rockets accompanied the balls, filling the air for fifteen minutes with these missiles of terror. The two batteries nearest the river directed their fire against McCarty's house, some hundreds of yards behind our front line, where Jackson and his staff had their headquarters. In less than ten minutes more than one hundred balls, rockets, and shells struck the house. Bricks, splinters of wood, and broken furniture were sent flying in all directions, making the premises dangerously untenable. General Jackson and his staff occupied the house at the time; yet, strange to say, not a person was even wounded. There is no account that the old hero "ingloriously fled," but it is in evidence that he retired with commendable dispatch to a safer place.

Though the batteries of the enemy were in a better position, on a lower plane, and with a narrower front than those of the Americans, the gunners of the latter fired with more precision and effect on this day, and on other occasions, as their own officers afterward admitted. In an hour's time the fire from the enemy's side began to slacken, and continued to abate until noon, when his two batteries to the right were abandoned. Our balls dismounted several of his guns early in the day, and in the afternoon the greater part of his artillery was dismounted or unfit for service. The carriages of three of the guns on the American side were broken, and two caissons, with over one hundred rounds of ammunition, were blown up by rockets, at which the enemy loudly cheered. The cheeks of the embrasures of our batteries were formed of cotton bales, which the enemy's balls struck, sending the cotton flying through the air. The impression that Jackson's breastwork line was constructed of bales of cotton is a mistake. Bales of cotton were used only at the bottom and sides of the embrasures, for a firmer support for the artillery, beneath a casing of heavy plank. The British, in the absence of cotton bales, used hogsheads of sugar, which were conveniently near, for the same purposes. These our shot easily knocked to pieces, saturating the damp earth around with the saccharine sweets. Our breastworks were more substantially and easily made of the alluvial earth.

The guns of the British batteries nearest the levee were directed in part against the marine battery across the river during the day, but with little effect. Before the close the enemy's guns were silenced, and several of them abandoned. The British columns were in readiness, drawn up in several parallel lines, prudently awaiting in the back ditches and the trenches between the batteries a favourable moment to advance to an assault of our lines. In this they were disappointed; the superiority of the American artillery left them no hope of an advantage by breaching our lines with this arm. That this was their object their own authorities state. The losses this day of the Americans were thirty-five killed and wounded; the enemy admitted a loss of seventy-five. During the night of the first of January, the latter succeeded in removing his heavy guns from the dismantled batteries, dragging them off with much difficulty through the mired earth.

Chapter 15

From the Enemy's Standpoint

It is interesting to view a situation from an enemy's standpoint, and to know the impressions made upon an enemy's mind in a great issue like the one of contest. We quote again from Gleig's Campaigns of the English Army:

It was Christmas Day, and a number of officers, clubbing their scant stocks of provisions, resolved to dine together in memory of former times. But at so melancholy a Christmas dinner, I do not remember to have been present. We dined in a barn; of table-ware, of viands, and of good cookery, there was a dismal scarcity. These were matters, however, of minor thought; the want of many well-known and beloved faces thrilled us with pain. While sitting at the table, a loud shriek from outside startled the guests. On running out, we found that a shot from the enemy's ship had cut almost in twain the body of a soldier, and he was gasping in death.

On the twenty-eighth, the British army advanced in full force, supported by ten pieces of artillery, with a view to a final assault. They did not do much more than the bringing on of a heavy artillery duel, in which they were severely worsted and driven back to camp. That the Americans are excellent shots, as well

73

with artillery as with rifles, we had frequent cause to acknowledge; but perhaps on no occasion did they assert their claim to the title of good artillerymen more effectually than on the present. Scarcely a shot passed over, or fell short; but all striking full into our ranks, occasioned terrible havoc. The crash of the fire-locks and the fall of the killed and wounded, caused at first some confusion. In half an hour three of our heavy guns were dismounted, many gunners killed, and the rest obliged to retire. The infantry advanced under a heavy discharge of round and grape shot, until they were checked by a canal in front. A halt was ordered, and the men commanded to shelter themselves in a wet ditch as best they could.

Thus it fared with the left of the army. The right failing to penetrate through the swamp, and faring no better, was compelled to halt. All thought of a general attack for this day was abandoned. It only remained to withdraw the troops from their perilous position with as little loss as possible. This was done, not in a body, but regiment by regiment, under the same discharge which saluted their approach.

There seemed now but one practicable way of assault; to treat these field-works as one would treat a regular fortification, by erecting breaching batteries against them, and silencing, if possible, their guns. To this end three days were employed in landing heavy cannon, bringing up ammunition, and making other preparations, as for a siege. One half of the army was ordered out on the night of the thirty-first, quietly led up to within three hundred yards of the enemy's works, and busily employed in throwing up a chain of works. Before dawn, six batteries were completed, with thirty pieces of heavy cannon mounted, when the troops, before the dawn of day, fell back and concealed themselves behind some thick brush in the rear. The Americans had no idea of what was going on until morning came. This whole district was covered with the stubble of sugar-cane, and every storehouse and barn was filled with large barrels containing sugar. In throwing up the works this sugar was used. Rolling the hogsheads towards the front, they were placed in the parapets of the batteries. Sugar, to the amount of many thousand pounds sterling, was thus disposed of.

On the morning of January 1st, a thick haze obscured the sun, and all objects at the distance of a few yards, for some hours. Finally, as the clouds of fog drifted away, the American camp was fully exposed to view, but three hundred yards away. The different regiments were upon parade, and presented a fine appearance. Mounted officers rode to and fro, bands were playing, and colours floating in the air. All seemed gala, when suddenly our batteries opened. Their ranks were broken; the different corps dispersing, fled in all directions, while the utmost terror and disorder appeared to prevail.

While this consternation lasted among the infantry, their artillery remained silent; but soon recovering confidence, they answered our salute with great precision and rapidity. A heavy cannonade on both sides continued during the day, until our ammunition began to fail—our fire slackening, while that of the enemy redoubled. Landing a number of guns from their flotilla, they increased their artillery to a prodigious amount. They also directed their cannon on the opposite bank against the flank of our batteries, and soon convinced us that all endeavours to surpass them in this mode of fighting would be useless. Once more, we were obliged to retire, leaving our heavy guns to their fate. The fatigue of officers and men, it would be difficult to form a conception of. For two entire nights and days not a man had closed his eyes, except to sleep amid showers of cannon-balls. We retreated, therefore, baffled and disheartened. It must be confessed that a murmur of discontent began to be heard in the camp. The cannon and mortars of the enemy played on our men night and day, from their main position; likewise a deadly fire from eighteen pieces on the opposite bank swept the entire line of our encampment. The duty of a picket was as dangerous as to go into battle. The American sharpshooters harassed them from the time they went on duty till they were relieved; while to light fires served only as marks for the enemy's gunners. The murmurs were not of men anxious to escape from a disagreeable situation; but rather resembled the growlings of a chained animal, when he sees his adversary, but can not reach him. All were eager to bring matters to the issue of a battle, at any sacrifice.

CHAPTER 16

Tennessee and Kentucky
Troops Arrive

General Carroll's division of Tennessee troops arrived about this time; also the Louisiana militia were reinforced by several companies from the more distant parishes. On the fourth of January the entire body of Kentucky militia reached New Orleans, twenty-two hundred in number, and went into camp on Prevost's plantation. The day following, seven hundred and fifty of these repaired to the lines, and went into camp in the rear, arms being furnished to but five hundred of the number. There were, at this time, nearly two thousand brave and willing men within Jackson's lines, whose services were lost to the army and to the country for the want of arms. The dangerous delay of the arrival of the troops, and with this, the failure of the arrival of the arms and munitions necessary to equip the men for service, had their beginning in the culpable negligence of the War Department at Washington, of which history has had occasion to complain. But a more immediate cause for the irreparable delay in the arrival of the stores for arming and equipping the troops is found in the conduct of the quartermaster who superintended the shipment of the same from Pittsburgh. Though he was offered a contract to ship these supplies by a steamboat, and to deliver them at New Orleans in ample time for use, for some reason he declined the offer. He then had them loaded on a flatboat and slowly floated to their destination, when there was little or no hope of their arrival in time for use. At the date of the final battle at New Orleans they were afloat somewhere near the mouth of the Ohio River, and of course did not arrive until many days after all need of them was over.

On the twenty-ninth of December, General Jackson wrote to the Secretary of War these words of protest against this failure to make provision for his army in such a crisis as the present:

I lament that I have not the means of carrying on more offensive operations. The Kentucky troops have not arrived, and my effective force at this point does not exceed three thousand men. That of the enemy must be at least double; both prisoners and deserters agreeing in the statement that seven thousand landed from their boats.

When the militia of Kentucky were called for, Governor Shelby was assured that the United States quartermaster would furnish transportation for the troops to New Orleans; but no such officer reported himself, and no relief came from Washington. The men had rendezvoused on the banks of the Ohio in waiting, and here the expedition must have ended had not Colonel Richard Taylor, of Frankfort, then quartermaster of the State militia, on his own credit, borrowed a sum sufficient to meet the immediate emergency. With this he purchased such boats as he could, some of which were unfit for the passage. Camp equipage could not be had in time, and about thirty pots and kettles were bought at Louisville, one to each company of eighty men. At the mouth of the Cumberland River they were detained eight days, with their axes and frows riving boards with which to patch up their old boats. From this point they started with half a supply of rations, to which they added as they could on the way down the Mississippi River. The men knew there was due them an advance of two months' pay when ordered out of the State. The United States quartermaster distributed this pay to the Tennessee troops who had preceded them, but withheld it from the Kentuckians. Believing that they would be furnished suitable clothing or pay, blankets, tents, arms, and munitions with reasonable promptness, they left home with little else than the one suit of clothing they wore, usually of homespun jeans. As a writer has said:

> Rarely, if ever, has it been known of such a body of men leaving their homes, unprovided as they were, and risking a difficult passage of fifteen hundred miles in the crudest of barges to meet an enemy. They could have been prompted alone by a patriotic love of country and a defiance of its enemies.

This contribution of Kentucky for the defence of Louisiana was made just after she had furnished over ten thousand volunteer troops in the campaigns of Harrison in the Northwest, who made up the larger part of the soldiers in that army for the two years previous, and who recently had won the great victory at the battle of the Thames. Governor Shelby tendered to the government ten thousand more Kentuckians for the army of the Southwest, if they were needed to repel the invaders.

It was in the midst of an unusually severe winter in Louisiana, in a season of almost daily rainfalls, when the Kentucky and part of the Tennessee troops reached their destination. They went into camp without tents or blankets or bedding of straw even, on the open and miry alluvial ground, with the temperature at times at freezing point. This destitution and consequent suffering at once enlisted the attention and sympathies of the public. The Legislature of Louisiana, in session, promptly voted six thousand dollars for relief, to which the generous citizens added by subscription ten thousand dollars more. With these funds materials were purchased. The noble women of New Orleans, almost without an exception, devoted themselves day and night to making up the materials into suitable garments and distributing them as they were most needed. In one week's time the destitute soldiers were supplied and made comfortable. These backwoodsmen, defenders of their country, did not forget till their dying day the generous and timely ministries in a time of trial, in which the women and the men of Louisiana, and especially of New Orleans, seemed to vie; nor did they cease to speak in their praise.

Again, in view of the approaching battle, Jackson, in correspondence with the Secretary of War, complains that the arms from Pittsburgh had not yet arrived, expressing grave apprehensions of the consequences. "Hardly," said he, "one third of the Kentucky troops, so long expected, are armed; and the arms they have are barely fit for use." He presages that the defeat of our armies and the dishonour of the officers commanding, and of the nation, may be consequences chargeable to the neglect of the government.

The American batteries on both sides of the river continued day and night to fire upon and harass the British. Wherever a group of the latter appeared, or an assailable object presented, the American fire was directed to disperse or destroy. This incessant cannonading exercised our gunners in the more skilful use of their pieces, annoyed the enemy in the work of his fortifications, and rendered his nights well-nigh sleepless.

CHAPTER 17

Jackson's Entrenched Line

Jackson's lines, five miles below the city, were along the canal, or old mill-race, on the border of the plantations of Rodrique and Chalmette. The old ditch, unused for years, had filled up in part with the washings of the earth from its sides, and grown over with grass. It was chosen because it lay at a point the shortest in distance from the river to the swamp, and thus the more easily defended. Along the upper bank of the canal a parapet was raised, with a banquet behind to stand upon, by earth brought from the rear of the line, thus raising the original embankment. The opposite side of the canal was but little raised, forming a kind of glacis.

Plank and posts from the adjacent fencing were taken to line the parapet and to prevent the earth from falling back into the canal. All this was done at intervals of relief, by the different corps, assisted by labour from the plantations near. It was not until the seventh of January that the whole extent of the breastwork was proof against the enemy's cannon.

The length of the line was less than one mile, more than half of which ran from the river to the wood, the remainder extending into the depths of the wood, taking an oblique direction to the left and terminating in the impassable swamp. The parapet was about five feet in height and from ten to twenty feet thick at the base, extending inland from the river one thousand yards. Beyond that, to the wood and swamp, where artillery could not well be employed, the breastwork was formed of a double row of logs, laid one over the other, leaving a space of two feet, which was filled with earth.

The artillery was distributed on the line as follows:

Battery 1	Captain Humphries United States artillery	consisted of two twelve-pounders and a howitzer, on field carriages, and was located thirty yards from the river, outside the levee
Battery 2	Lieutenant Norris Navy	ninety yards from Battery 1; one twenty-four pounder
Battery 3	Captains Dominique & Bluche Baratarians	fifty yards from Battery 2; two twenty-four pounders
Battery 4	Captain Crawly Navy	twenty yards from Battery 3; one thirty-two pounder, served by part of the crew of the *Carolina*
Battery 5	Colonel Perry & Lieutenant Carr Artillery	one hundred and ninety yards from Battery 4; two six-pounders
Battery 6	Lieutenant Bertel	thirty-six yards from Battery 5; one brass twelve-pounder
Battery 7	Lieutenants Spotts & Chauveau	one hundred and ninety yards from Battery 6; one eighteen and one six-pounder
Battery 8		sixty yards from Battery 7; one brass carronade, next Carroll's and Adair's commands

Out beyond this last piece the line formed a receding elbow, mentioned above, made unavoidable by great sinks in the soil, filled with water from the canal. Here, and beyond into the wood, the ground was so low that the troops were literally encamped in the water, walking often in mire a foot in depth, their few tents being pitched on small mounds surrounded with water or mud. Amid these discomforts, in this ague-breeding miasma, the Tennesseans, under Generals Coffee and Carroll, and the Kentuckians, under General Adair, for days endured the dangers of battle and privations of camp and campaign. As one historian who was with Jackson's army writes:

> They gave an example of the rarest military virtues. Though constantly living and sleeping in the mire, these patriotic men never uttered a complaint or showed the least symptoms of impatience. It was vitally necessary to guard that quarter against an attack on our flank, and to repulse him on the edge of our breastwork, where artillery could not be employed. We had no battery on the centre and left for thirteen hundred yards, the nature of the ground not admitting. The Tennesseans and Kentuckians defended this entire two thirds of our line with rifles and muskets only. As anticipated, the enemy made his main assault against these rifles and muskets, in a vain attempt to flank our army.

A view of the positions of the respective corps in Jackson's line will be of interest here. The redoubt on the river, where the right of the line rested, was guarded by a company of the Seventh United States Infantry, commanded by Lieutenant Ross; the artillery was served by a detachment of the Forty-fourth United States Infantry, under Lieutenant Marant. At the extremity of the line, between Battery 1 and the river, was posted Captain Beale's company of New Orleans Rifles, thirty men strong. The Seventh United States Regiment covered the space from Batteries 1 to 3, four hundred and thirty men, commanded by Major Peire. The interval between Batteries 3 and 4 was occupied by Major Plauche's battalion of Louisiana uniformed companies, and by Major Lacoste's battalion of Louisiana men of colour, the former two hundred and eighty-nine men, and the latter two hundred and eighty strong. From Batteries 4 to 5, the line was held by Major Daquin's battalion of St.

ANDREW JACKSON, 7TH PRESIDENT OF THE UNITED STATES

Domingo men of colour, one hundred and fifty in number; and next to these were placed the Forty-fourth United States Regulars, two hundred and forty men, commanded by Colonel Baker.

From this point toward the centre and left, for eight hundred yards, the breastwork was manned by the troops from Tennessee, commanded by General Carroll, and the Kentuckians, under command of General Adair, supported by the men of the nearest batteries. General Carroll reported that he had over one thousand Tennesseans in his immediate command, in line of action. General Adair had, on the morning of the seventh of January, received arms for only six hundred of the Kentucky troops. He says, in a subsequent correspondence, that on the seventh, anticipating the attack of the British the following day, he went into New Orleans, and plead with the Mayor and Committee of Safety to lend him, for temporary use, several hundred stand of arms stored in the city armoury and held for the defence of the city in emergency, and to put a check to any possible insurrectionary disturbance. To this the Mayor and committee finally consented, on the condition that the removal of the arms out of the city should be kept secret from the public. To this end, instead of General Adair marching in and arming his men, the city authorities had the arms, concealed in boxes, hauled out to the camp and delivered there. This was done late in the dusk of the evening, and on the night of the seventh four hundred more of the Kentuckians were thus armed and marched forward to take a position with their comrades just in the rear of the entrenchment, making one thousand Kentuckians under arms and ready for tomorrow's battle.

In council with General Jackson, General Adair had suggested that the British would most probably endeavour to break our line by throwing heavy columns against it at some chosen point; and that such was the discipline of their veterans, they might succeed in the effort without very great resistance was made. To be prepared for such a contingency, it would be well to place a strong reserve of troops centrally in the rear of the line, ready at a moment's notice to reinforce the line at the point of assault. Jackson approved this suggestion, and gave orders to General Adair to hold the Kentucky troops of his command in position for such contingency. With Colonel Slaughter's regiment of seven hundred men, and Major Reuben Harrison's battalion, three hundred and five men (the Kentuckians under arms), Adair took position just in the rear of Carroll's Tennesseans, occupying the centre of the breastwork line.

By the statements of their commanders, the joint forces of the Tennesseans and Kentuckians defending the left centre were about two thousand men. General Coffee's Tennesseans, five hundred in number, occupied the remainder of the line on the left, which made an elbow-curve into the wood, terminating in the swamp. Ogden's squad of cavalry and a detachment of Attakapas dragoons, about fifty men in all, were posted near the headquarters of the commander-in-chief, and these were later joined by Captain Chauvau, with thirty mounted men from the city. The Mississippi cavalry, Major Hinds in command, were held in reserve, one hundred and fifty strong, posted on Delery's plantation. Detachments of Colonel Young's Louisiana militia, in all about two hundred and fifty men, were placed on duty at intervals on the skirts of the wood, behind the line as far as Piernas' Canal. Four hundred yards in the rear a guard was posted to prevent any one going out of the camp, and a line of sentinels was extended to the wood for the same purpose.

The above details show that there were of Jackson's army on the left bank of the river, on active duty, about forty-six hundred men; yet on the battle-line of the eighth of January there were less than four thousand to engage the enemy. The remainder were in reserve, or on guard duty at various points.

From official reports and historical statements derived from British sources, there were present and in the corps of the British army of assault, on the morning of the eighth of January, about eleven thousand men, fully eight thousand of whom were in the attacking columns and reserve on the left bank of the river, the flower of the English army.

CHAPTER 18

The Battle of 8th of January

It was not yet daybreak on the morning of the eighth of January when an American outpost came hastily in, with the intelligence that the enemy was in motion and advancing in great force. In brief time, as the day began to dawn, the light discovered to our men what seemed the entire British army in moving columns, occupying two thirds of the space from the wood to the river. Obedient to the commands of their officers, who gallantly led in front of their men, the massive columns of the enemy moved up with measured and steady tread. Suddenly a Congreve rocket, set off at a point nearest the wood, blazed its way across the British front in the direction of the river. This was the signal for attack. Immediately the first shot from the American line was fired from the twelve-pounder of Battery 6. This was answered by three cheers from the enemy, who quickly formed in close column of more than two hundred men in front and many lines deep. These advanced in good order in the direction of Batteries 7 and 8, and to the left of these. It was now evident that the main assault would be made upon that part of the breastwork occupied by Carroll's Tennesseans, with the intent to break the line here and flank Jackson's army on the right.

As soon in the morning as word came that the British

were in motion for an advance, General Adair formed his Kentuckians in two lines in close order, and marched them to within fifty paces of the breastwork, in the rear of Carroll's command. The day had dawned, and the fog slowly lifted. There was no longer doubt of the point of main assault, as the enemy's heaviest columns moved forward in Carroll's front. The lines of the Kentucky troops were at once moved up in order of close column to the Tennesseans, deepening the ranks to five or six men for several hundred yards. Batteries 6, 7, and 8 opened upon the enemy when within four or five hundred yards, killing and wounding many, but causing no disorder in his ranks nor check to his advance. As he approached in range, the terrible fire of rifles and musketry opened upon him from the Tennessee and Kentucky infantry, each line firing and falling back to reload, giving place to the next line to advance and fire.

The British attack was supported by a heavy artillery fire, while a cloud of rockets continued to fall in showers throughout the contest. The assaulting columns did little execution with small arms, as they came up relying more on the use of the bayonet in case of effecting a breach in our line. Some of them carried fascines and ladders in expectation of crossing the ditch and scaling the parapet. But all in vain. The musketry and rifles of the Tennessee and Kentucky militia, joining with the fire of the artillery, mowed down whole files of men, and so decimated their ranks as to throw them into a panic of disorder and force a retreat. This first disastrous repulse was within twenty-five minutes after the opening of the battle. Writers present who have undertaken to describe the scene at the time say that the constant rolling fire of cannon and musketry resembled the rattling peals of thunder following the lightning flashes in a furious electric storm. An English officer present mentions the phenomenon, that though the flashes of the guns were plainly visible in front, the firing seemed to be from the wood and swamp a mile or two away on the left. They did not hear the sound from the front, but only the echoes from the direction named, as though the battle raged out there.

The defeated column, forced to fall back broken and disordered, was finally rallied by the heroic efforts of the officers, reinforced with fresh troops, and led to a second attempt at assault; but the carnage and destruction were as great as in the first attempt, while almost no impression was made upon the defensive line of the Americans. The British were again compelled to retreat in disorder, leaving great numbers of their comrades dead or wounded on the ground, or prisoners to the Americans. The hope of victory had now become a forlorn one to the British. They were broken in numbers, broken in order and discipline, and broken in prestige. Yet the brave officers, led by their commanders-in-chief, determined not to give up the contest without a last desperate effort. A part of the troops had dispersed and retreated to shelter among the bushes on their right; the rest retired to the ditch where they were first perceived in the morning, about five hundred yards in our front. In vain did the officers call upon the men to rally and form again for another advance, striking some with the flat of their swords, and appealing to them by every incentive. They felt that it was almost certain destruction to venture again into the storm of fire that awaited them, and were insensible to everything but escape from impending death. They would not move from the ditch, and here sheltered the rest of the day. The ground over which they had twice advanced and twice retreated was strewn thickly with their dead and wounded. Such slaughter of their own men, with no apparent loss on our side, was enough to appal the bravest of mankind.

Nearly one hundred of the enemy reached the ditch in front of the American breastwork, half of whom were killed and the other half captured. A detachment of British troops had penetrated into the wood toward our extreme left, to divert attention by a feint attack. The troops under General Coffee opened on these with their rifles, and soon forced them to retire.

After the main attack on the American left and centre had begun, another column of over twenty-five hundred men, under the command of General Keene, advanced along the road near the levee, and between the levee and the river, to attack the American line on the extreme right. They were partly sheltered by the levee from the fire of the artillery, except that of Battery 1 and the guns across the river. Our outposts were driven in, and the head of the column pushing forward occupied the unfinished redoubt in front of our entrenched line before more than two or three discharges of artillery could be made. Overpowering the small force here, they compelled it to fall back, after killing and wounding a few men. Bravely led by Colonel Rence and other officers of rank, the British gained a momentary advantage, and threatened to storm the entrenchment itself. But Beale's Rifles from the city, defending this extreme, poured fatal volleys upon the head of the column, while Batteries 1 and 2 mowed down the ranks. The Seventh Regiment, the only infantry besides Beale's in musket range, did deadly execution also. By these, the farther advance of the enemy was made impossible, while the nearest ground they occupied was strewn with their dead and wounded, among whom were General Keene, Colonel Rence, and other prominent officers. Many passed the ditch and scaled the parapet only to be shot down in the redoubt by the unerring riflemen behind the entrenched line. Like the main column on the left, this second column on the right, broken and shattered, was compelled to fall back in great disorder upon the reserve, with no effort after to renew the assault. The dead and wounded lay thick along the road, the levee, and the river bank, as far out as the range of our guns. A flanking fire from the battery across the river harassed the troops in this column both in the advance and retreat, as they passed in plain view, from which fire they sustained severe losses.

The battle was now ended as far as the firing of musketry and small arms was concerned. The last volleys from these ceased one hour after the British column first in motion attacked our line upon the left centre, at half-past seven o'clock. In that brief time, one of the best equipped and best disciplined armies that England ever sent forth was defeated and shattered beyond hope by one half its number of American soldiers, mostly militia. For one hour after the opening attack the firing along the American line had been incessant, and the roar of the cannon, mingling with the rattling noise of the musketry and rifles, reverberated over the open plains and echoed back from the wood and swamp, until the issue of combat sent the enemy to cover beyond range. The artillery from our batteries, however, kept up a continuous fire against the guns of the enemy, or against squads of their troops who might expose themselves, until two o'clock in the afternoon, when the lull of strife came to all.

The scene upon the field of contest was one that can not be pictured in words to convey an adequate impression. British officers who campaigned in Europe, in the wars of the Peninsula, testified that in all their military experiences they had witnessed nothing to equal the stubborn fierceness of the contending forces, and the fearful carnage that befell the troops of the British army. We have mentioned how thickly strewn was the ground along the levee and the road, on the right next to the river, with the dead and the wounded of the enemy. The fatality among the officers here was fearful. General Keene, in command of this second attacking column, was borne from the field badly wounded. Colonel Rence, next in command with Keene, was killed while leading the assault in the redoubt. Nearby fell Major King, mortally wounded, and others of rank, leaving the command with but few leaders to conduct the broken ranks in precipitate retreat. On our left, in the front of the Tennesseans and Kentuckians, the greatest execution had been done. The slaughter here was appalling. Within a space three hundred yards wide, and extending out two hundred yards from our breastwork on the battlefield, an area of about ten acres, the ground was literally covered with the dead and desperately wounded. A British officer, who became also historian, says that under the temporary truce he rode forward to view this scene. Such a one he never witnessed elsewhere. There lay before him in this small compass not less than one thousand men, dead or disabled by wounds, all in the uniform of the British soldier; not one American among the number. The fatality to the English officers had been even greater on our left than on our right. Lord Pakenham, commander-in-chief, after the first repulse of the main column, with a courage as reckless as it was vain rode forward to rally his troops and lead them to a second attack in person, and in the midst of a hail of missiles from cannon and small-arms fell mortally hurt with several wounds, and died within an hour. Major-General Gibbs, next in command, was stricken down a few minutes after, dying within a few hours. Others in high rank were carried down in the holocaust of casualties, until the British army became unnerved for the want of leadership in the hour of disaster and peril.

Adjutant-general Robert Butler, in his official report to General Jackson a few days after the battle of the eighth, placed the losses of the British at seven hundred killed, fourteen hundred wounded, and five hundred prisoners; twenty-six hundred men, or almost one third the entire number the enemy admitted to have taken part in the contest of the day. The loss of the Americans was six killed and seven wounded, thirteen in all. Instead of comment upon this remarkable disparity of losses, and the causes that led to such a signal victory for the Americans and such a humiliating defeat for our enemies, it will be more interesting to our readers to quote from English writers who were participants in the battle, and eye-witnesses of the scenes they describe with graphic pen. We are ever curious to know what others see and say of us, especially if they honestly criticize us with a spice of prejudice.

CHAPTER 19

8th January—an English Account of the Battle

Gleig, in his *History of British Campaigns*, says:

Dividing his troops into three columns, Sir Edward Pakenham directed that General Keene, at the head of the Ninety-fifth, the light companies of the Twenty-first, Fourth, and Forty-fourth Regiments, and the two black corps, should make a demonstration on the right; that General Gibbs, with the Fourth, Twenty-first, Forty-fourth, and Ninety-third, should force the enemy's left; while General Lambert, with the Seventh and Forty-third, remained in reserve. Our numbers now amounted to a little short of eight thousand, a force which, in any other part of America, would have been irresistible. The forces of the enemy were reported at twenty-three to thirty thousand. I suppose their whole force to have been twenty-five thousand. All things were arranged on the night of the 7th, for the 8th was fixed upon as the day decisive of the fate of New Orleans.

On the morning of the 8th, the entire army was in battle array. A little after daylight, General Pakenham gave the word to advance The troops on the right and the left, having the Forty-fourth to follow with the fascines and ladders, rushed on to the assault. On the left, next to the river, a detachment of the Ninety-fifth, Twenty-first and Fourth, stormed a three-gun battery and took it. It was in advance of the main line of works. The enemy, in overpowering numbers, repulsed our attacking force and recaptured the battery *with immense slaughter*. On our right again, the Twenty-first and Fourth being almost cut to pieces, and thrown into some confusion by the enemy's fire, the Ninety-third pushed up and took the lead. Hastening forward, our troops soon reached the ditch; but to scale the parapet without ladders was impossible. Some few indeed, by mounting upon each others' shoulders, succeeded in entering the works; but these were, most of them, instantly killed or captured. As many as stood without were exposed to a sweeping fire, which cut them down by whole companies. It was in vain that the most obstinate courage was displayed. They fell by the hands of men they could not see. The Americans, without lifting their faces above the rampart, swung their fire-locks over the wall and discharged them directly upon their heads.

Poor Pakenham saw how things were going, and did all that a general could do to rally his broken troops. He prepared to lead them on himself, when he received a slight wound in the knee, which killed his horse. Mounting another, he again headed the Forty-fourth, when a second ball took effect more fatally, and he dropped lifeless in the arms of his *aid-de-camp*. Bravely leading their divisions, Generals Gibbs and Keene were both wounded, and borne helpless from the field. All was now confusion and dismay. Without leaders, and ignorant of what was to be next done, the troops first halted, and then began to retire, till finally, the retreat was changed into a flight, and they quitted the ground in the utmost disorder. But the retreat was covered in gallant style by the reserve. The Seventh and Forty-third, under General Lambert, presented the appearance of a renewed attack, and the enemy, overawed, did not pursue.

On the granting of a two-days' truce for the burial of the dead, prompted by curiosity, I mounted my horse and rode to the front. Of all the sights I ever witnessed, that which met me there was, beyond comparison, the most shocking and the most humiliating. Within the compass of a few hundred yards, were gathered together nearly a thousand bodies, all of them arrayed in British uniforms. Not a single American was among them; all were English. And they were thrown by dozens into shallow holes, scarcely deep enough to hide their bodies. Nor was this all. An American officer stood by smoking a cigar, and abruptly counting the slain with a look of savage exultation, repeating that their loss amounted only to eight killed and fourteen wounded. I confess that, when I beheld the scene, I hung down my head half in sorrow, and half in anger. With my officious informant, I had every inclination to pick a quarrel. But he was on duty, and an armistice existed, both of which forbade. I turned my horse's head and galloped back to the camp.

The changes of expression now visible in every countenance, no language can portray. Only twenty hours ago, and all was hope and animation; wherever you went, you were enlivened by the sounds of merriment and raillery. The expected attack was mentioned, not only in terms of sanguine hope, but in perfect confidence as to the result. Now gloom and discontent everywhere prevailed. Disappointment, grief, indignation and rage succeeded each other in all bosoms; nay, so were the troops overwhelmed by a sense of disgrace, that, for awhile they retained their sorrow without hinting at the cause. Nor was this dejection because of laurels tarnished, wholly. The loss of comrades was to the full, as afflicting as the loss of honour; for, out of more than seven thousand in action on this side, no fewer than two thousand had fallen. Among these were two generals in chief command, and many officers of courage and ability. Hardly an individual survived who had not to mourn the loss of some special and boon companion.

CHAPTER 20

British Excuses for Defeat

Many causes for the failure of the campaign of invasion, and for the disastrous issue of the battle of the eighth, were conjectured in the English army. Almost universal blame was attributed to Colonel Mullins, of the Forty-fourth Regiment, which was detailed under orders to prepare and have ready, and to carry to the front on the morning of the eighth, fascines and ladders with which to cross the ditch and scale the parapet, as the soldiers fought their way to the breastwork of the Americans. It was freely charged that the Colonel deserted his trust and at the moment of need was half a mile to the rear. It was then that Pakenham, learning of Mullins' conduct, placed himself at the head of the Forty-fourth and endeavoured to lead them to the front with the implements needed to storm the works, when he fell mortally wounded. Of this incident another British officer, Major B.E. Hill, writes:

Before sunset of the 7th, I was directed to carry instructions to Colonel Mullins, of the 44th, respecting the redoubt in which the fascines and scaling ladders were placed, and to report the result of my interview to Sir Edward Pakenham. I saw Colonel Mullins, and read to him the directions from headquarters, begging to know if he thoroughly understood their purport?

I was assured that nothing could be clearer. Reporting to Sir Edward, he thanked me for so completely satisfying him that the orders so important would be certainly and well executed.

Colonel Mullins may have been guilty of conduct unbecoming an officer, for which he was tried and cashiered in England; he probably saved his life at the expense of his honour, in being absent from his post on that day. But the British officers magnified the importance of the presence of himself and his regiment with their fascines and ladders ready for use. Even with the help of these devices, there were not men enough in the English army to have crossed the ditch, climbed the parapet, and made a breach in the breastwork line of the Americans. Some of them might have reached the ditch alive, as did some of their comrades, but like those comrades they would have died in the ditch or been made prisoners. The Americans, too, could have used the bayonet as well as the British, if necessary.

CHAPTER 21

8th January—West Bank
of the River

We have mentioned that after the night battle of the twenty-third of December General Jackson ordered General Morgan to move his command of Louisiana troops from English Turn, seven miles below the British camp at Villere's, and to take a position on the west bank of the Mississippi, opposite to the American camp. Very naturally, the possibility, and even the probability, of the enemy, when his army was made formidable by all the reinforcements coming up, throwing a heavy flanking force across the river, marching it to a point opposite New Orleans and forcing a surrender of the city, suggested itself to the military eye of Jackson. After the latter entrenched at Rodrique Canal, by the first of January, there was no other strategical route by which the British could have successfully assailed the city. The importance of this seems to have been fully comprehended neither by the one combatant nor the other until too late to fully remedy the omission.

Just such a flanking movement was undertaken by the English at the latest day, which brought on a second battle on the eighth, on the right bank of the river, resulting in a defeat to the American forces, and well-nigh ending in disaster to the American cause. It is in evidence that this strategic movement was the result of a council of war held by the British officers, at which Admiral Sir Alexander Cochrane was present. This idea of reaching the city by a heavy detachment thrown across the river and marching up to a point opposite, in cannon reach, had occurred before; but the difficulty was in finding a way to cross over the troops and artillery, with the Americans in command of the means of transportation. The suggestion came from Admiral Cochrane that the Villere Canal from the bayou could be easily deepened and widened to the river bank and opened into the river for the passage of the boats and barges from the fleet, and a sufficient force thrown across the river in that way under cover of night. This seemed feasible, and the strategy determined on. It is related further that Lord Pakenham insisted that the main attack upon the city for its capture should be made by a heavy detachment in this direction, and at the same time only a demonstration in force made on the American breastworks with the whole army, supported by the artillery. He urged that to directly assault the fortified line in front would be at a fearful loss of life, if successful; if it failed it would be disastrous. The Admiral replied to this tauntingly, that there was no cause for alarm over anticipated defeat; he would undertake to force the lines of the American militia with two or three thousand marines. In allusion to this, Latour says:

> If the British commander-in-chief was so unmindful of what he owed to his country, and to the army committed to his charge, as to yield to the ill-judged and rash advice of the Admiral, he sacrificed reason in a moment of irritation; though he atoned with his life for having acted contrary to his own judgment.

Undoubtedly the English made their last and most fatal blunder here.

As the English writers who were with the army have so variously minimized the forces under Colonel Thornton, and so exaggerated the numbers of the Americans in this affair on the west bank, we quote from the official report of Major-General Lambert, who succeeded to the immediate command of the invading army after the fall of Generals Pakenham, Gibbs, and Keene, what appears to be reliable:

To Lord Bathurst
January 10th, 1815

It becomes my duty to lay before your Lordship the proceedings of the force lately employed on the right bank of the Mississippi River. Preparations had been made on our side to clear out and widen the canal that led from the bayou to the river, by which our boats had been brought up to the point of disembarkation, and to open it to the Mississippi, by which our troops could be got over to the right bank, and the cooperation of armed boats be secured. A corps consisting of the 85th light infantry, two hundred seamen, four hundred marines, the 5th West India Regiment, and four pieces of artillery, under the command of Colonel Thornton, of the 85th, were to pass over during the night, and move along the right bank toward New Orleans, clearing its front, until it reached the flanking battery of the enemy on that side, which it had orders to carry. Unlooked for difficulties caused delay in the entrance of the armed boats from the canal into the river, destined to land Colonel Thornton's corps, by which several hours' delay was caused. The ensemble of the general movement was lost, a point of the last importance to the main attack on the left bank, although Colonel Thornton ably executed his instructions.

Major-General Lambert
Commanding

The two regiments above, with the seamen and marines, if all were present, would have given Colonel Thornton a command of nearly two thousand men. But it is said that in consequence of some difficulties in getting the boats through the canal into the river, and delay consequent thereon, a part of the forces were left behind. From the best authorities, there were twelve hundred British troops landed upon the west bank of the river on the morning of the eighth, by daybreak—all except the West India regiment.

CHAPTER 22

Defences and Forces on the West Bank

General Morgan, commanding the Louisiana militia, was in position on Raquet's old canal site, next to the river. Major Latour, chief of the engineer corps, had been instructed by General Jackson, a week or two before the battle, to proceed across the river and to select on that side a suitable line for defensive works for General Morgan, in case the enemy should attempt a flanking movement on the right bank. Of this mission, Major Latour writes:

> Agreeable to orders, I waited on General Morgan, and in the presence of Commodore Patterson communicated to him my orders, and told him I was at his disposal. The General seemed not to come to a conclusion, but inclined to make choice of Raquet's line. He then desired that I inspect the different situations myself, and make my report to him. My orders were to assist him, and my opinion was subordinate to his.
>
> I chose for the intended line of defence an intermediate position, nearly at equal distances from Raquet's and Jourdan's canal, where the wood inclines to the river, leaving a space of only about nine hundred yards between the swampy wood and the river.

Works occupying this space could not well be turned, without a siege and assault in heavy force by the enemy. I made a rough draft of the intended line, and immediately the overseer set his negroes to execute the work. Returning to the left bank, I made my report to the Commander-in-chief, who approved the disposition made.

One thousand men could have guarded a breastwork line here, and half that number would have been sufficient had pieces of cannon been mounted in the intended outworks. That line, defended by the eight hundred troops and the artillery of General Morgan's command, on the 8th, could have defied three or four times the number of British who crossed over to the right bank that day. But these dispositions had been changed by General Morgan, and the negroes ordered to work on the Raquet line.

Major Latour had selected for General Jackson his line of defence on the left bank of the river, and had directed the construction of the breastwork and redoubts to the entire satisfaction of the General. He objected to the Raquet line favoured by General Morgan, as wholly unsuited for defence. The space here from the river to the wood swamp was two thousand yards, or considerably over one mile, a much longer line than Jackson's on the other side. To be effective against an attacking force, the entrenchment and outworks must be extended to cover the entire space. It would require then more than double the number of troops and of pieces of artillery for defence than the situation selected by Latour.

In determining on this change of the line of defence, contrary to the judgment and warning of the chief of the engineer corps, General Morgan seems to have been influenced by one consideration paramount to all others. He was in daily council with Commodore Patterson, and was assured of the powerful aid of his battery on the right bank, which had done such execution in the ranks of the British across the river. Should the enemy attack General Morgan's position at Raquet's line, the Commodore could turn his twelve pieces of cannon in their embrasures, sweep the field, and drive back any reasonable force in range. With this support of his artillery, the few hundred militia of Morgan's command could more successfully repulse an attack at Raquet's line than at the line selected by Latour farther away. This change in the situation and plan of defence is characterized by Latour and other authorities as an unmilitary proceeding, as it abandoned the idea of a fortified line behind which a successful defence could have been made probable, if not certain, for an almost open field subject to the flanking movement of veteran troops against raw militia, with no auxiliary support except a park of artillery with guns turned another way, and of most doubtful use in case of need. General Morgan must not share alone the criticism which has been so freely made of his disposition of forces and changes of strategic plans which resulted in sensational disaster to his command. Commodore Patterson, experienced in military affairs as well as naval, advised with him, and must have approved. This change of line, made some days before the eighth, must have been known, and on the representations of Morgan and Patterson, approved by General Jackson. It is not conceivable that so important a change of plans would have been made by a subordinate officer, affecting seriously the safety of New Orleans, without the consent of the commander-in-chief. The latter seemed always to have held in very high personal esteem these two officers, and to have had confidence in their abilities as commanders.

As mentioned above, the dispositions made for a line of defence by Major Latour were changed by General Morgan, and the negroes set to work on Raquet's line. A breast-work fortification was thrown up by the seventh of January, extending but two hundred yards from the river bank out on the site of the old canal. From this terminus across the plantation land to the wooded swamp was an open plain, with scarce an obstruction to the deploy of troops or the sweep of artillery. The old canal had long been in disuse, and the ditch was filled nearly full with the washings and deposits of years. Behind this two hundred yards of entrenchment General Morgan massed all the Louisiana troops of his command and planted his artillery, three pieces in all. From the end of the breastwork on the right, one mile or eighteen hundred yards to the swamp, there were no defensive works from behind which to repulse the assault of an enemy, nor any means of resistance in sight to an attack, other than the guns in battery of Commodore Patterson, of more than doubtful use, and the yet very doubtful contingent of reinforcements sufficient from General Jackson's limited supply of men and arms.

On the seventh, the forces of Morgan's immediate command were the First Louisiana Militia on the left, next to the river; on the right of these, the Second Louisiana; and on the right of the latter, the drafted Louisiana militia, in all about five hundred men, who occupied the fortified line of two hundred yards. It was not until late this day that General Jackson seemed to fully awaken to the impending dangers of this formidable flanking movement across the river. He at once gave orders that five hundred of the unarmed Kentucky militia in camp should be marched up the river to New Orleans and receive certain arms in store there; then cross the river, and march down five miles on the west bank and reinforce General Morgan's command by, or before, daylight next morning. It was late afternoon when they started on this tramp of ten miles, through mud and mire ankle deep. Arriving at New Orleans, it was found that four hundred stand of arms which were expected to be obtained from the city armoury had been loaned to General Adair, and sent to him at the Kentucky camp for other use. From other sources some miscellaneous old guns were obtained to equip less than two hundred of the detailed Kentuckians, who crossed the river, began their weary night march, and reported to General Morgan before daylight of the eighth, ready for duty, though they had not slept for twenty-four hours, nor eaten anything since noon of the previous day. Their arms, a mongrel lot, were many of them unfit for combat; old muskets and hunting-pieces, some without flints, and others too small-bored for the cartridges.

Chapter 23

The Battle and Retreat

About sunset on the evening of the seventh, General Morgan was notified of the intention of the enemy to cross the river by Commodore Patterson, who had closely observed his movements in the afternoon. Before day-dawn on the eighth, the General received information of the enemy landing on the west bank, at Andry's plantation. The rapid current of the Mississippi had carried his little flotilla three miles below the point he had desired to land. Having debarked his troops, he marched up the river; his boats, manned by four pieces of artillery, keeping abreast and covering his flank. A detachment of Louisiana militia, about one hundred and fifty men, under command of Major Arnaud, had been sent in the night a mile or two down the river to oppose the landing and to check the advance of the British. These raw militia, very poorly armed, retired before the enemy. The detachment of one hundred and seventy Kentuckians just arrived, under command of Colonel Davis, was ordered to move forward to the support of the command of Major Arnaud. Though wearied with the toilsome all-night march, the Kentucky troops went forward about one mile below Morgan's line and took position on Mayhew's Canal, their left resting on the bank of the river. Major Arnaud halted his Louisiana militia on the right of these in line. The enemy, over one thousand strong, came up in force under Colonel Thornton, who commanded the British in the night battle of the twenty-third. A heavy fire of musketry from the front was supported by a flanking fire of artillery and rockets from the boats. The command of Major Arnaud gave way and hastily retreated to the wood, appearing no more during the day on the field of action. The Kentuckians returned the fire of the enemy with several effective volleys, when they were ordered by an *aid-de-camp* of General Morgan's, just arrived, to fall back and take a position on his line of defence.

The falling back of the Kentuckians before the enemy was under orders which they could not but obey. They were holding him in check and inflicting heavier losses than they were receiving, against four or five times their own numbers. They fell back one mile in good order. By disposition of the commanding officer, they were placed in line, with an open space of two hundred yards between their extreme left and the extreme right of the entrenched Louisianians, and stretched out to cover a space of three hundred yards, or one man to nearly two yards of space. The remainder of the line stretching to the wood on the extreme right, twelve hundred yards, was wholly without defensive works, or any defence excepting a picket of eighteen men under Colonel Caldwell, stationed out two hundred yards beyond the extreme right of the Kentuckians. Less than two hundred poorly armed militia were thus isolated and distributed in thin ranks to defend a line one mile in length, while General Morgan lay behind his entrenchment, defending a space of two hundred yards with five hundred troops and three pieces of artillery, which could have been easily held by two hundred men.

Colonel Thornton, in command of the British troops, in advancing to the attack, readily perceived with his trained military eye the vulnerable situation of the American forces. Gleig, the English author present, gives the disposition of the enemy's assaulting columns as follows: The Eighty-fifth, Colonel Thornton's own regiment, about seven hundred men, stretched across the field, covering our front, with the sailors, two hundred in number, prepared to storm the battery and works; while the marines formed a reserve, protecting the fleet of barges. It is not probable that the attack upon the entrenchments next to the river was intended to be more than a demonstration in force to hold the attention of General Morgan and his command there, while the main assault was being directed with the Eighty-fifth Regiment against the thin and unsupported line of the Kentucky militia, with a view of flanking these and getting in the rear of General Morgan's breastworks.

We quote from Major Latour's *Historical Memoir* a further account:

> The enemy advancing rapidly by the road opposite the left of the line, the artillery played on him with effect; and as he came nearer, the musketry began to fire also. This having obliged him to fall back, he next directed his attack against the detached Kentuckians on our right, one column moving toward the wood and the other toward the centre of the line. Now was felt the effect of the bad position that we occupied. One of the enemy's columns turned our troops at the extremity of Colonel Davis' command, while the other penetrated into the unguarded space between the Kentuckians and the breastwork of the Louisianians. Flanked at both extremes by four times their own number, and unsupported, the Kentucky militia, after firing several volleys, gave way; nor was it possible again to rally them. Confidence had vanished, and with it all spirit of resistance. If instead of extending

over so much space, those troops had been formed in close column, the confusion that took place might have been avoided, and a retreat in good order made.

The enemy having turned our right, pushed on towards the rear of our left, which continued firing as long as possible. At length the cannon were spiked just as the enemy arrived on the bank of the canal. Commodore Patterson had kept up an artillery fire on the British over the river. As they advanced up the road, he would now have turned his cannon in their embrasures, and fired on those of the enemy who had turned our line and come in range. But the Kentucky troops and the Louisianians masked the guns, and made it impossible to fire without killing our own men. Seeing this, he determined to spike his guns and retreat.

The Louisiana militia under General Morgan now fell back and took a position on the Bois Gervais line, where a number of the fleeing troops rallied. A small detachment of the enemy advanced as far as Cazelards, but retired before evening. In the course of the night all the enemy's troops recrossed the river, to join their main body. The result of this attack of the enemy on the right bank was, the loss of one hundred and twenty of his men, killed and wounded. The commander-in-chief, receiving intelligence of the retreat of our troops on the right bank, ordered General Humbert, formerly of the French army, who had tendered his services as a volunteer, to cross over with a reinforcement of four hundred men, assume command, and repulse the enemy, cost what it might. The order was verbal; some dispute having arisen over the question of military precedence, and the enemy withdrawing, no further steps were taken.

Chapter 24

Ingloriously Fled

In this historic review, we dwell exhaustively upon the episode of this battle on the west bank, on the 8th of January, 1815, not because of any intrinsic importance of the subject, but rather from the sensational incidents which attended the movements of the belligerents, and which were consequent upon the issue. The galling words of General Jackson, hastily and unguardedly uttered in an attempt to throw the blame of defeat upon a small detachment of Kentucky militia, "the Kentuckians ingloriously fled," were resented as an undeserved stigma upon the honour and good name of all the Kentuckians in the army, and upon the State of Kentucky herself. The epigrammatic phrase, construed to mean more than was intended, perhaps, like Burchard's *Rum, Romanism, and Rebellion*, struck a chord of sympathetic emotion that vibrated not only in the army and the community of Louisiana, but throughout the entire country. These burning words are of record in the archives at Washington, and remembered in history; but the facts in full, which vindicate the truth and render justice to whom it is due, are known to but few, if known to any now living. In the words of Latour:

> What took place on the right bank had made so much sensation in the immediate seat of war, and had

been so variously reported abroad, to the disparagement of many brave men, that I thought it a duty incumbent on me to inquire into particulars and trace the effect to its cause.

Rather than give our own impressions, we quote from Reid and Eaton's *Life of Jackson* an account of this affair, interesting because written when the subject was yet fresh in the public mind, and from the intimacy of the authors with the personal and public life of General Jackson:

On the night of the 7th, two hundred Louisiana militia were sent one mile down the river, to watch the movements of the enemy. They slept upon their arms until, just at day, an alarm was given of the approach of the British. They at once fell back towards General Morgan's line. The Kentucky detachment of one hundred and seventy men, having arrived at five in the morning, after a toilsome all-night march, were sent forward to cooperate with the Louisiana militia, whom Major Davis met retreating up the road. They now formed behind a mill-race near the river. Here a stand was made, and the British advance checked by several effective volleys. General Morgan's aid-de-camp being present, now ordered a retreat back to the main line of defence, which was made in good order. In the panic and disorderly retreat afterwards are to be found incidents of justification, which might have occasioned similar conduct in the most disciplined troops. The weakest part of the line was assailed by the greatest strength of the enemy. This was defended by one hundred and seventy Kentuckians, who were stretched out to an extent of three hundred yards, unsupported by artillery. Openly exposed to the attack of a greatly superior force, and weakened by the extent of ground they covered, it is not deserving reproach that they abandoned a post they had strong reasons for believing they could not maintain. General Morgan reported to General Jackson the misfortune of defeat he had met, and attributed it to the flight of these troops, who had drawn along with them the rest of his forces. True, they were the first to flee; and their example may have had some effect in alarming others. But, in situation, the troops differed. The one were exposed and enfeebled by the manner of their arrangement; the other, much superior in numbers, covered a less extent of ground, were defended by an excellent breastwork manned by several pieces of artillery; and with this difference,—the loss of confidence of the former was not without cause. Of these facts, Commodore Patterson was not apprised; General Morgan was. Both reported that the disaster was owing to the flight of the Kentucky militia. Upon this information, General Jackson founded his report to the Secretary of War, by which these troops were exposed to censures they did not merit. Had all the circumstances as they existed, been disclosed, reproach would have been prevented. At the mill-race no troops could have behaved better; they bravely resisted the advance of the enemy. Until an order to that effect was given, they entertained no thought of retreating.

Intelligence quickly came to General Jackson of the defeat and rout of General Morgan's command, imperilling the safety of the city of New Orleans, in the midst of the congratulations over the great victory of the main army on the east bank. Naturally, a state of intense excitement followed, bordering on consternation for a few hours. When the danger was ended by the withdrawal of the British forces to recross the river, the report of General Morgan, followed by that of Commodore Patterson, came to headquarters, laying the blame of defeat and disaster to the alleged cowardly retreat of the Kentucky militia. With General Jackson's great personal regard for the authors of these reports, he took for granted the correctness of the charge of censurable conduct. Amid the tumult of emotions that must have been felt, rapidly succeeding the changes of scenes and incidents and issues of strategy and battle during that eventful twenty-four hours, the great commander yielded to the impulse of the moment to write in his official report to the Secretary of War, on the ninth, the day succeeding the battles, the following words:

Simultaneously with his advance upon my lines, the enemy had thrown over in his boats a considerable force to the other side of the river. These having landed, were hardly enough to advance against the works of General Morgan; and what is strange and difficult to account for, at the very moment when their discomfiture was looked for with a confidence approaching to certainty, the Kentucky reinforcement, in whom so much reliance had been placed, ingloriously fled, drawing after them by their example the remainder of the forces, and thus yielding to the enemy that most formidable position. The batteries which had rendered me, for many days, the most important service, though bravely defended, were of course now abandoned; not, however, until the guns had been spiked.

Commodore Patterson also sent in a report to the Secretary of the Navy, characterizing the little detachment of Kentucky militia in terms as censurable and as unjust as were the words of General Jackson. When these official reports became publicly known, imputing all blame of disaster to the retreat of the Kentuckians, an indignant protest was entered by General Adair and by the entire Kentucky contingent of the army. In this protest they had the sympathy and support of a large portion of other troops of the army, and of the community. Language at this late day of forgetfulness and calmer reason would be too tame to really portray the irritations, the bitter recriminations, and the angry protests which agitated army circles, and the civil community as well, and which were echoed from many parts of the country at large.

CHAPTER 25

A Court of Inquiry

General Adair, supported by the officers of his command, insisted that the statements made in these reports to the departments at Washington were made upon a misapprehension of the facts, and that great injustice had been done the Kentucky militia in General Morgan's command by attempting to shift the responsibility of defeat from its real sources, and placing it to their discredit.

A military court of inquiry was demanded, and granted by the commander-in-chief, the members of which were officers of rank in the army, and disinterested by their relations in the findings, and General Carroll, of Tennessee, appointed to preside. The following notice was served on General Morgan, and similar notices on other officers concerned:

New Orleans, La.
February 9, 1815
Brigadier-General Morgan

Sir: A Court of Inquiry is now in session for the purpose of inquiring into the conduct of the officers under your command, on the morning of the 8th of January. As you are somewhat concerned, I have to request that you will introduce such witnesses on tomorrow as you may think necessary. The conduct of Colonel Cavalier, and of Majors Tesla and Arnaud, is yet to be inquired into.

Your Most Obedient Servant,

Wm. Carroll

Major-General

President of Court

The following opinion was rendered:

Report of the Court of Inquiry
Headquarters
7th Military District
New Orleans, La.
February 19, 1815
General Orders

At a Court of Inquiry, convened at this place on the 9th inst., of which Major-General Carroll is President, the military conduct of Colonel Davis, of Kentucky Militia, and of Colonels Dijon and Cavalier, of Louisiana Militia, in the engagement on the 8th of January last, on the west bank of the Mississippi, were investigated; the Court, after mature deliberation, is of opinion that the conduct of those gentlemen in the action aforesaid, and retreat on the 8th of January, on the western bank of the river, is not reprehensible. The cause of the retreat the Court attributes to the shameful flight of the command of Major Arnaud, sent to oppose the landing of the enemy. The retreat of the Kentucky militia, which, considering their position, the deficiency of their arms, and other causes, may be excusable; and the panic and confusion introduced into every part of the line, thereby occasioning the retreat and confusion of the Orleans and Louisiana militia. While the Court found much to applaud in the zeal and gallantry of the officer immediately commanding, they believe that a further reason for the retreat may be found in the manner in which the force was placed on the line; which they consider exceptionable. The commands of Colonels Dijon, Cavalier, and Declouet, composing five hundred men, supported by three pieces of artillery, having in front a strong breastwork, occupying a space of only two hundred yards; whilst the Kentucky militia, composing Colonel Davis' command, only one hundred and seventy strong, occupied over three hundred yards, covered by a small ditch only.

The Major-General approves the proceeding of the Court of Inquiry, which is hereby dissolved.
By Command
H. Chotard
Assistant Adjutant-General

CHAPTER 26

Controversy Between Jackson and Adair

General Adair seems to have regarded the decision of the Court of Inquiry as a modifying compromise, in deference to the high personal character and influence of a number of persons concerned, and not the full vindication of the Kentucky militia from the imputations of ungallant conduct on the field reflected upon them in the official reports. The controversy, and other causes preceding it, had rankled the bosoms of both General Jackson and himself, and estranged the warm friendship that had before existed between them. Adair thought that Jackson should withdraw, or modify, the language of his official report. General Jackson was not a man to readily retract; and was certainly not in the humour with Adair to retract anything he had said. He would do no more than approve the opinion of the Court of Inquiry. This, perhaps, was as much as General Adair should have asked at the time.

On the 10th of February, 1816, the Legislature of Kentucky, in a resolution of thanks to General Adair for gallant services at New Orleans, added:

And for his spirited vindication of a respectable portion of the troops of Kentucky from the libellous imputation of cowardice most unjustly thrown upon them by General Andrew Jackson.

This and other incidents intensified the animosity of feeling.

It was some two years after the close of hostilities that the correspondence between Jackson and Adair was terminated in language and spirit so intensely bitter as to make the issue personal. Adair had reported all proceedings and facts concerning the Kentucky troops during the campaign to Governor Shelby, who had taken a very active part in sending all possible aid for the defence of New Orleans. In these reports he reflected on what he deemed the injustice done the Kentucky troops in several official publications; especially by General Jackson, not only in the affair of Morgan's rout, but in his report of other operations during the campaign. These were causes of irritation on the part of the commander-in-chief. The burning words in the reports of General Jackson, General Morgan, and Commodore Patterson, imputing cowardice to a few of their comrades, had touched a sensitive chord and sunk deep into the hearts of the Kentucky troops in the army. In their resentments, expressed in words and sometimes in actions, all danger from the enemy being over, they were perhaps not always so orderly as soldiers should be while in camp, or on scout or picket service.

In the closing correspondence, the language used by both Jackson and Adair became exceedingly bitter; that of the former beyond all restraint toward his respondent. The issue of this controversy, tradition says, was a challenge to meet upon the field of honour, then so called, and to settle it at the pistol's point. The challenge was accepted. By whom it was sent, the author has not been able to learn. In the absence of any record, written or in print, of this affair, he has to rely upon oral recitals which have come down

JOHN ADAIR, 8TH GOVERNOR OF KENTUCKY

through members of the Adair family in Kentucky, and are remembered in the main facts today. The would-be combatants met by appointment at a spot selected on the border line of their respective States, accompanied each by his second, his surgeon, and a few invited friends. The unfriendly breach between Jackson and Adair, and its possible tragic issue, seems to have given deep concern to some of their friends. There was no other cause of enmity between them save what grew out of the unfortunate occurrences at New Orleans. They were of the same political party—Jeffersonian Republicans, as they were known then, in distinction from Federalists. Jackson had won renown and prestige as no other in America, and his name had already been mentioned in connection with the highest office within the gift of the people. Adair was held in high esteem by the people of Kentucky, and bright hopes of political preferment were held out by his party friends. Other considerations added, induced friends on either side to urge a reconciliation, which was happily effected on terms mutually satisfactory. The above account of this meeting on the field of honour was related to the author by General D.L. Adair, of Hawesville, Kentucky, now long past his fourscore years. He gave the facts to the writer, he said, as he received them from his father, Doctor Adair, of Hardin County, Kentucky, many years ago. Doctor Adair was a cousin of General Adair, of Jackson's army, and was one of the intimate friends whom the General invited to be present upon the ground.

The correspondence of Jackson and Adair throws light upon the subject of this controversy, and reveals to us some of the causes of the errors and contentions of this affair. We have mentioned that Adair, in his eagerness to arm as many as possible of the Kentucky militia and place them in line for the main battle of the eighth, went into the city and plead with the Committee of Safety to loan him four hundred stand of arms, held in the city armoury for the protection of New Orleans, for a few days. This urgent request was granted, and the arms privately moved out, hauled to the camp of the Kentuckians, and delivered there about nightfall of the seventh. Four hundred more of the Kentuckians were thus armed and moved up to the rear of the breastwork, ready for the battle next morning. Adair believed that he was acting in the line of his duty, and that Jackson would approve of his device for arming more of his idle men in camp. Busy as he was that day in New Orleans, and in equipping and marshalling the men of his command for battle, he was not made aware of the urgent need of reinforcements on the opposite bank of the river, nor did he know of the purpose of the commander-in-chief to arm these from the city armoury. While Adair's device very much strengthened Jackson's line on the left bank, it unfortunately defeated Jackson's plan of sending four hundred more men to reinforce General Morgan on the right bank, and may in this way have largely contributed to the latter's defeat.

When Jackson, late on the seventh, ordered a detail of five hundred of the Kentucky militia to be marched at once to New Orleans, there to be armed, to cross the river and report by daylight to General Morgan, he expected to use the arms from the city armoury. There was no other supply.

We may readily imagine the feeling of disappointed chagrin and passion that stirred to its depths the strong nature of Jackson, when the intelligence quickly came to him across the river of the disaster to Morgan's command, and of its retreat toward New Orleans, followed by the enemy. It was in this tumult of passion and excitement that the report of Morgan, followed by that of Patterson, was brought to him, imputing the cause of defeat and disaster to the cowardly retreat of the Kentucky detachment. Under the promptings of these incidents of the day, Jackson's report to the Secretary of War was made, in which the words of censure were so unjustly employed. Jackson must have informed Morgan on the evening of the seventh that he would reinforce him with five hundred armed soldiers. When Colonel Davis reported to Morgan, one hour before daylight, the arrival of the Kentucky contingent, the latter was expecting five hundred men to reinforce him. Had this been done, the Kentucky troops and Major Arnaud's one hundred and fifty Louisianians would have made the forces sent to the front to check the advance of the British under Colonel Thornton over six hundred men. Such a force, well officered, would probably have held the enemy in check, fallen back in good order, and made a stubborn fight on the line of battle. But there was only one third the Kentucky force expected; and when Major Arnaud's command retreated, there was but this contingent of one hundred and seventy Kentucky militia left to resist the advance of one thousand British veterans, and to meet their main assault on the centre and right of the long line of battle. It made its march from New Orleans at midnight, and was reported to General Morgan before daybreak. These facts give a more intelligible view of the plan of battle arranged by this officer. It was undoubtedly marred and broken up by the unforeseen incidents mentioned, unfortunately for General Morgan and for the American cause. Commodore Patterson, in his report to the Secretary of the Navy, five days after the battle, makes the force of Kentucky militia that gave way before the British four hundred men, more than double the real number; thus showing the error prevalent.

When the facts came out that General Adair had secured the four hundred stand of city arms for his own immediate command with which Jackson had designed to arm the reinforcement for General Morgan, the incident was naturally very irritating to the Commander-in-chief. It was imputed as a cause, in part, of the defeat and disaster on the right bank. Jackson seems to have complained to Adair that the latter ought to have known of his order to call out the detachment of five hundred Kentuckians in time, and of his intention to arm them in the city. Adair replied that the order came to General Thomas, in chief command of the Kentuckians, lying ill in camp, while he was busily engaged in New Orleans and at the front, preparing his own command for battle next day; that he did not know of the intention of Jackson to use the city arms until too late to repair the mistake. It made up a chapter of accidents and errors, happening with best intentions. As for the little body of Kentucky militia, who were made sensationally notorious, where there was honour and fame for no one, poorly armed and wearied with fasting and a heavy all-night march, they did as well as troops could do. It is doubtful if any one hundred and seventy troops in Jackson's army would have done better. Unsupported, and attacked and flanked by four times their own number, no troops could have held their ground longer.

In the possession of Judge William H. Seymour, of New Orleans, is an original letter of Major Latour, addressed to General Morgan in anticipation of the publication of his "Historical Memoirs of the War of 1812-15," advising him that he would give an account also of the military situation and battle on the west bank, as he viewed them; and inviting any statement from General Morgan in his own vindication that he might choose to make. This letter is not printed in the history, but was seen and copied by the author, through the courtesy of Judge Seymour, who is a lineal descendant of a sister of Andrew Jackson. A diligent inquiry was made by the writer of this monograph for a copy of General Morgan's report, and also of letters or documents from him in vindication of his course in the affairs mentioned. If any such are in print, or otherwise preserved, the author did not succeed in finding them, to his regret.

New Orleans, La.
April, 1815
To General David Morgan

Sir: I send you herewith a copy of the publication that I am preparing for the press, upon the last campaign, relating to the transaction that took place on the right bank, on the 8th of January.

As I am of opinion that you are to bear the blame of our disgrace on that part of our defence, I thought myself in duty bound, as a man of honour, to participate to you what I wrote on the subject previous to my putting it to the press. What I have stated is, I believe, strictly true; however, sir, you are in a situation to furnish me with such observations as may tend to rectify what should not be printed, in its true light.

Be persuaded, sir, that I have no enmity against you; on the contrary, as a private citizen, I have the regard for you that I think you deserve. Then I hope you will not take my conscientious caution in a bad part, and that you will direct to me in Philadelphia, where I am departing for in a day or two, anything you will choose to write for your vindication. It will find room in the appendix, at all events, should it be founded upon proper authorities.

I remain, sir, your most respectful servant,
A. Lacarriere Latour

Incidental prominence has been given to this episode of the battle of the eighth, on the west bank of the river, far beyond its real merits as an event of the military operations around New Orleans. Worse panic and confusion resulted among the American militia at Bladensburg, in front of Washington, and at other places, during the War of 1812–15, and passed into history without unusual criticism, as incidents common to warfare. But the injustice done to the little band of Kentucky militia, imputing to them cowardly conduct, on the part of some of the highest officials of the army, aroused a spirit of indignant protest that echoed far and wide, and would not down. Had it not been for the misleading report of General Morgan, followed by that of Commodore Patterson, and prompting that of General Jackson to the Secretary of War, saying that "the Kentuckians ingloriously fled," and imputing blame to no other party, the incident of the battle and defeat would have been mentioned and passed without comment.

CHAPTER 27

The Covert Retreat of the British

The battles of the eighth were decisive of the campaign, and of the War of 1812-15, so far as military operations were concerned. The British had been beaten in generalship and beaten upon the field of battle, until they were made to feel and to confess to defeat so crushing as to leave no hope of retrieving disaster. Within fifteen days after landing, they had sustained losses equal to one third of their entire army of invasion. With prestige gone and spirit broken, and their ranks shattered, there was but one thing left to do. To cover their retreat and get safely back to their ships before the broken remnants of their army were made to capitulate by surrender became a matter of gravest concern. The situation is set forth in the following official letter to the Secretary of War:

Camp Below New Orleans
January 19, 1815

Sir: Last night, at 12 o'clock, the enemy precipitately decamped and returned to his boats, leaving behind him, under medical attendance, eighty of his wounded, fourteen pieces of heavy artillery, and a quantity of ammunition. Such was the situation of the ground he abandoned, and that through which he retired, protected by canals, redoubts, entrenchments, and swamps on his right and the river on his left, that I could not, without great risk, which true policy did not seem to require, much annoy him on his retreat.

Whether it is the purpose of the enemy to renew his efforts at some other point, or not, I can not certainly determine. In my own mind, however, there is little doubt that his last exertions have been made in this quarter, at least for the present season. In this belief I am strengthened by the prodigious losses he has sustained at the position he has just quitted, and by the failure of his fleet to pass Fort St. Philip. His loss on this ground, since the debarkation of his troops, as stated by the last prisoners and deserters, and as confirmed by many additional circumstances, must have exceeded four thousand men. We succeeded on the 8th, in getting from the enemy about one thousand stand of arms of various kinds.

Since the action of the 8th, the enemy have been allowed but very little respite, my artillery from both sides of the river being constantly employed until the hour of their departure, in annoying them. They were permitted to find no rest.

I am advised by Major Overton, who commands at Fort St. Philip, in a letter of the 18th, that the enemy having bombarded his fort for nine days, with thirteen-inch mortars, without effect, had on the morning of that day retired. I have little doubt that he would have sunk their vessels had they attempted to run by.

Do not think me too sanguine in the belief that *Louisiana* is now clear of the enemy. I need not assure you, however, that wherever I command, such a belief shall never occasion any relaxation in the measures for resistance. I am but too sensible that while the enemy is opposing us, is not the most proper time to provide for them. On the 18th, our prisoners on shore were delivered to us, an exchange having been agreed to. I shall have on hand an excess of several hundred.

I have the honour to be, &c.

Andrew Jackson

Commander-in-Chief.

The losses to the American army, in the five battles fought from the twenty-third of December to the eighth of January, inclusive, are summarized in the report of the Adjutant-general, which we give:

Camp Below New Orleans
January 16, 1815

Sir: I enclose for the information of the War Department, a report of the killed, wounded, and missing, of the army under Major-General Jackson, in the different actions with the enemy since their landing.

Robert Butler

Adjutant-General

Battle	Killed	Wounded	Missing
December 23rd	24	115	74
December 28th	9	3	0
January 1st	11	23	0
January 8th	13	39	19
Totals	57	185	93

A total of three hundred and thirty-five men. This includes the killed, wounded, and missing in the two battles on the eighth.

Our English authorities are so marked with exaggerations and discrepancies as to numbers in either army, and also as to losses and casualties, that they are unreliable. There is with nearly all their writers, and in the reports of their officers, a disposition to minimize numbers on their own side, and to overstate those on the side of the Americans. This was no doubt due to a sense of mortified pride and deep chagrin over their repeated defeats and final expulsion from the country, under humiliations such as English armies and navies had rarely before known in history. General Jackson was not far wrong in estimating the entire losses of the British, during the two weeks of invasion, at more than four thousand men. If the large number who deserted from their ranks after the battles of the eighth of January be included, the excess would doubtless swell the numbers much above four thousand. Their killed, wounded, and missing on the eighth approximated three thousand. So decimated and broken up were their columns that they dared not risk another battle.

CHAPTER 28

Repulse of the British Fleet Before Fort St. Philip

On the first of January, Major W. H. Overton, in command of Fort St. Philip, which guards the passage of the Mississippi River from its mouth for the protection of New Orleans, received information that the enemy intended to capture or pass the fort, to cooperate with their land forces threatening the city. On the seventh, a fleet of two bomb-vessels, one sloop, one brig, and one schooner appeared and anchored below the fortification and began an attack. For nine days they continued a heavy bombardment from four large sea-mortars and other ordnance, but without the effect they desired. Making but little impression toward destroying the fort, and fearing to risk an attempt finally to pass our batteries, the fleet withdrew on the morning of the eighteenth, and passed again into the Gulf. Our loss in this affair was but two killed and seven wounded. During the nine days of attack the enemy threw more than one thousand bombs from four ten-and thirteen-inch mortars, besides many shells and round shot from howitzers and cannon.

CHAPTER 29

An English View of Defeat

A graphic pen-picture of the chaotic and wretched condition of the English army after the crushing defeat of the eighth, and until its final return to the fleet, is given by Gleig in his *Narrative of the Campaigns*. It will be read with all the more interest because it is the frank admission of a brave though prejudiced officer, giving an enemy's view of the great disaster that befell the British arms, in which he fully shared:

General Lambert prudently determined not to risk the safety of his army by another attempt upon works evidently so much beyond our strength. He considered that his chances of success were in every respect lessened by the late repulse. An extraordinary degree of confidence was given to the enemy, while our forces were greatly diminished in numbers. If again defeated, nothing could save our army from destruction; it could only now retreat in force. A retreat, therefore, was resolved upon while the measure appeared practicable, and toward that end all our future operations were directed.

One great obstacle existed; by what road were the troops to travel to regain the fleet? On landing, we had taken advantage of the bayou, and thus come within two miles of the cultivated country, in our barges. To return by the same route was impossible. In spite of our losses there were not enough boats to transport above one half of the army at one time. If we separated, the chances were that both divisions would be destroyed; for those embarked might be intercepted, and those left behind might be attacked by the whole American army. To obviate the difficulty, it required that we should build a passable road through the swamp, to Lake Borgne, some twenty miles away. The task was burdened with innumerable difficulties. There was no firm foundation on which to work, and no trees to assist in forming hurdles. All we could do was to bind together large quantities of swamp weeds and lay them across the quagmire. It was but the semblance of a road, without firmness and solidity.

To complete this road, bad as it was, occupied nine days, during which our army lay in camp, making no attempt to molest the enemy. The Americans, however, were not so inactive. A battery of six guns, mounted on the opposite bank, kept up a continued fire upon our men. The same mode of proceeding was adopted in front, and thus, night and day we were harassed by danger, against which there was no fortifying ourselves. Of the extreme unpleasantness of our situation, it is hardly possible to convey an adequate conception. We never closed our eyes in peace, for we were sure to be awaked before the lapse of many minutes, by the splash of a round shot or shell in the mud beside us. Tents we had none, but lay some in open air, and some in huts of boards, or any material we could procure. From the moment of our landing, December 23rd, not a man had undressed, except to bathe; many had worn the same shirt for weeks. Heavy rains now set in, with violent storms of thunder and lightning, and keen frosts at night. Thus we were wet all day, and nearly frozen at night. With our outposts there was constant skirmishing. Every day they were attacked by the Americans, and compelled to maintain their ground by dint of hard fighting. No one but those who belonged to this army can form a notion of the hardships it endured, and the fatigue it underwent.

Nor were these the only evils which tended to lessen our numbers. To our soldiers every inducement was held out by the enemy to desert. Printed papers, offering lands and money as the price of desertion, were thrown into the pickets, while individuals would persuade our sentinels to quit their stations. It could not be expected that bribes so tempting would always be refused. Many desertions began daily to take place, and ere long became so frequent, that the evil rose to be of a serious nature. In the course of a week, many men quitted their colours, and fled to the enemy.

Meanwhile, the wounded, except such as were too severely hurt to be removed, were embarked in the boats and sent off to the fleet. Next followed the baggage and stores, with the civil officers, commissaries, and purveyors; and last of all such of the light artillery as could be drawn without risk of discovery. But of the heavy artillery, no account was taken. It was determined to leave them behind, retaining their stations. By the 17th, no part of the forces was left in camp but the infantry. On the evening of the 18th, it also began the retreat. Trimming the fires, and arranging all in the order as if no change were to take place, regiment after regiment stole away, as soon as darkness concealed their motions, leaving the pickets to follow as a rear guard, with injunctions not to retire till daylight appeared. Profound silence was maintained; not a man opened his mouth, except to issue necessary orders in a whisper. Not a cough or any other noise was to be heard from the head to the rear of the column. Even the steps of the soldiers were planted with care, to prevent the slightest echo. Nor was this precaution unnecessary. In spite of every endeavour to the contrary, a rumour of our intention had reached the Americans; for we found them of late very watchful and prying.

While our route lay alongside the river, the march was agreeable enough, but as soon as we entered the marsh, all comfort was at an end. Our roadway, constructed of materials so slight, and resting on a foundation so infirm, was trodden to pieces by the first corps. Those who followed were compelled to flounder on the best way they could. By the time the rear of the column gained the morass, all trace of a way had disappeared. Not only were the reeds torn asunder and sunk by the pressure of those in front, but the bog itself was trodden into the consistency of mud. Every step sunk us to the knees, and sometimes higher. Near the ditches, we had the utmost difficulty in crossing at all. There being no light, except what the stars supplied, it was difficult to select our steps, or follow those who called to us that they were safe on the other side. At one of those ditches, I myself beheld an unfortunate wretch gradually sink until he totally disappeared. I saw him flounder, heard his cry for help, and ran forward with the intention of saving him; but before I had taken a second step, I myself sunk to my breast in the mire. How I kept from smothering is more than I can tell, for I felt no solid bottom under me, and sank slowly deeper and deeper, till the mud reached my arms. Instead of rescuing the poor soldier, I was forced to beg assistance for myself. A leathern canteen strap being thrown to me, I laid hold of it, and was dragged out, just as my fellow-sufferer was buried alive, and seen no more.

All night we continued our journey, toiling and struggling through this terrible quagmire; and in the morning reached the Fishermen's Huts, mentioned before as standing on the brink of Bayou Bienvenue, near Lake Borgne. The site is as complete a desert as the eye of man was ever pained by beholding. Not a tree or a bush grew near. As far as the eye could reach, an ocean of weeds covering and partially hiding the swamp presented itself, except on the side where a view of the Lake changed, without fertilizing, the prospect. Here we were ordered to halt; and perhaps I never rejoiced more sincerely at any order than at this. Wearied with my exertions, and oppressed with want of sleep, I threw myself on the chilly ground, without so much as pulling off my muddy garments; in an instant all my cares and troubles were forgotten. After many hours, I awoke from that sleep, cold and stiff, and creeping beside a miserable fire of weeds, devoured the last morsel of salt pork my wallet contained.

The whole army having come up, formed along the brink of the Lake; a line of outposts was planted, and the soldiers commanded to make themselves as comfortable as possible. But there was little comfort. Without tents or shelter of any kind, our bed was the morass, and our sole covering the clothes which had not quitted our backs for a month. Our fires, so necessary to a soldier's happiness, were composed solely of weeds, which blazed up and burned out like straw, imparting but little warmth. Above all, our provisions were expended, with no way to replenish in reach. Our sole dependence was the fleet, nearly one hundred miles away, at anchor. It was necessary to wait until our barges could make the trip there, and return. For two entire days, the only provisions issued to the troops were some crumbs of biscuit and a small allowance of rum. As for myself, being fond of hunting, I determined to fare better. I took a fire-lock and went in pursuit of wild ducks, of which there seemed plenty in the bog. I was fortunate enough to kill several, but they fell in the water, about twenty yards out. There was no other alternative. Pulling off my clothes, and breaking the thin ice, I waded out and got my game, and returned to shore, shivering like an aspen. As I neared the shore, my leg stuck fast in the mire, and in pulling it out my stocking came off, a loss that gave me great discomfort, until we went aboard the fleet. I request that I may not be sneered at when I record this loss of my stocking as one of the disastrous consequences of this ill-fated expedition.

As the boats returned, regiment after regiment set sail for the fleet. But, the wind being foul, many days elapsed before all could be got off. By the end of January, we were all once more on board our former ships. But our return was far from triumphant. We, who only seven weeks ago had set out in the surest confidence of glory, and I may add, of emolument, were brought back dispirited and dejected. Our ranks were woefully thinned, our chiefs slain, our clothing tattered and filthy, and our discipline in some degree injured. A gloomy silence reigned throughout the armament, except when it was broken by the voice of lamentation over fallen friends. The interior of each ship presented a scene well calculated to prove the misadventures of human hope and human prudence. On reaching the fleet, we found that a splendid regiment, the 40th Foot, of one thousand men, had just arrived to reinforce us, ignorant of the fatal issue of our attack. But the coming of thrice their number could not recover what was lost, or recall the fateful past. There was no welcome, nor rejoicing; so great was the despondency that no attention was given to the event. A sullen indifference as to what might happen next seemed to have succeeded all our wonted curiosity, and confidence of success in every undertaking.

On the 4th of February, the fleet weighed anchor and set sail, though detained by adverse winds near the shore of Cat Island until the 7th, when it put to sea. Our course, towards the east, led to the conjecture that we were steering towards Mobile. Nor was it long before we came in sight of the bay which bears that name.

CHAPTER 30

Second Attack on Fort Bowyer

So great and so repeated had been the reverses of the British arms, that an opportunity to retrieve lost prestige, even in a small degree, could not well be permitted to pass unimproved. The great flotilla of sixty vessels, with the fragments of the shattered army, which set sail with flags and pennants gaily flying in the breeze from Negril Bay, Jamaica, but a little over two months ago, was still a power upon the sea, at a safe distance from Jackson's triumphant army. The little outpost of a fort that guarded Mobile Bay, which had inflicted a heavy loss on, and beaten off, a squadron of the enemy's ships a few months before, lay in their path homeward, and it was determined to invest it, and to overwhelm it with numbers. On the sixth of February, the great armament appeared in sight of Dauphin Island. On the seventh, twenty-five ships anchored in a crescent position extending from the island toward Mobile Point, where stood the fort. On the morning of the eighth, the enemy landed five thousand troops opposite the line of ships at anchor, investing the fort by sea and land. The fortification was erected for defence mainly on the sea side, to render it formidable to ships attempting to enter the pass into Mobile Bay. On the land side was a sandy plain, rendering it incapable of defence against a superior force protected by extensive

143

siege works. The enemy mounted a number of batteries behind parapets and epaulements, which directed their fire upon the weakest parts of the defence. The fort was gallantly defended by a garrison of three hundred and fifty men, under command of Colonel William Lawrence. Some losses were inflicted on the besiegers as they continued to push their works to within short musket-range of the fort. But the heavy cannonading and fire from small-arms encircled the besieged from every direction, and further defence became hopeless. Terms of surrender were agreed to on the eleventh, and on the twelfth the garrison marched out with the honours of war, yielding possession to the enemy.

Chapter 31

Negotiations for Peace

The small victory at Mobile Bay was barren of any gain to the British cause; for, on the fourteenth, two days after the surrender, intelligence came from England to General Lambert that articles of peace had been signed by the plenipotentiaries of the belligerent nations, in session at Ghent. Gleig remarks, in his *Narrative*:

> With the reduction of this trifling work ended all hostilities in this quarter of America; for the army had scarcely reassembled, when intelligence arrived from England of peace. The news reached us on the fourteenth, and I shall not deny that it was received with much satisfaction.

On the nineteenth, General Jackson issued an address from headquarters, from which we reproduce as follows:

> The flag-vessel, which was sent to the enemy's fleet at Mobile, has returned and brings with it intelligence, extracted from a London paper, that on the twenty-fourth of December articles of peace were signed by the commissioners of the two nations.

Thus, on the day after the first landing of the British army on Louisiana soil, and after the first battle was fought at night, terms of peace were agreed on. It was fifteen days after that auspicious event until the battles on the eighth occurred, causing such disaster and loss of valuable lives to the English army and nation; and fifty-two days from the signing of articles until a message of the good news was received by the commander-in-chief of the British forces. There was no alternative but to await the slow passage of the ship across the wide Atlantic, with sails set to breeze and calm, and sometimes tossed and delayed by adverse storm. Today, the news of such an event would be flashed over the great cables under the sea and the network of electric wires throughout the land, in the twinkling of an eye after its occurrence. Such an advantage at the time would have been worth to England the entire cost of the telegraph system of the world.

Legislature Suppressed

On the morning of the twenty-eighth of December, just as the British began their attack on the American line, General Jackson issued an order forcibly forbidding the meeting of the Legislature in session, and for taking possession of the legislative halls. The proceeding created great excitement in the civil and military circles of the city, especially among the members of the body and their immediate friends. The author is indebted to Mr. William Beer, of the Howard Library of New Orleans, for the loan of a copy of a rare little book entitled *Report of the Committee of Inquiry on the Military Measures Employed Against the Legislature of the State of Louisiana, the 28th of December, 1814.* In the full report of the testimony taken by the committee, we have a history of the causes which led to this open rupture between the commander-in-chief and the General Assembly of Louisiana, and of its incidents and issues.

Since the landing of the British army on the twenty-third, there were afloat in nebulous form some rumours of disaffection toward the American military occupation of Louisiana, among an element of the population unfriendly to the sovereignty of the United States over the territory since its purchase from Napoleon. Up to the time of the military occupation under Jackson, this hostile feeling seemed to display its temper and policies mainly in matters of civil procedure. There was very naturally a jealous opposition on the part of many leading citizens, of French and Spanish descent, of whom the population west of the Mississippi was almost entirely made up, against the annexation of the territory east of that river as part of Louisiana, on equal terms of citizenship and co-sovereignty. This east territory, they felt, had been rudely seized and possessed by the United States, against the claim and protest of Spain. It was being settled by American people, who in time would help to Americanize the country, and to lessen the power and control of the former Creole domination. The virtues of a patriotic love of their native countries yet lingered in the bosoms of these citizens—a patriotic love which, when finally transferred to the new government they were under, burned as brightly for the new sovereignty as for the old.

Captain Abner L. Duncan, aid to Jackson, testified before the committee as follows:

On the 28th, Colonel Declouet (of General Morgan's command) coming in haste from the city, joined this respondent and begged him to inform General Jackson that a plan was on foot among several members of the Legislature for the surrender of the country to the enemy. Colonel Declouet named in confidence to myself, to Generals Jackson and Morgan, and to Major Robinson, several members as persons determined on making the attempt. He added, that he heard one or more members say, that Jackson was carrying on a Russian war (alluding to the burning of Moscow), and that it was best to save private property by a timely surrender; that he, Colonel Declouet, had been invited to join in the measure. On this respondent making the communication to General

Jackson, the order he received was: "Tell Governor Claiborne to prevent this, and to blow them up if they attempt it!"

Colonel Declouet told me the plan had been first disclosed to him by the Speaker of the House, Mr. Guichard. He said in presence of General Jackson and Mr. Daresac, that many other influential men were concerned in it, and that they had held several night or secret meetings on the subject. He gave the names of Mr. John Blanque and Mr. Marigny, and generally all those voting with Mr. Blanque in the House. He stated that, as an inducement offered to unite in the plan, he was informed by Mr. Guichard that General Jackson would burn and destroy everything before him sooner than surrender the country, and that the English would respect private property. I understood also, from some members of the House, Mr. Harper and Mr. Fickland among them, and in the Senate from General Morgan and Mr. Hireart, that an attempt would be made to dismember the State. I also understood from other members that they would consider it an act of violence; and would resist it by violence.

Colonel Declouet was the chief informant at headquarters; but rumours had been rife for several days of disloyal utterances and of mysterious proceedings, which caused uneasiness to the civil and military authorities, and especially to Governor Claiborne, who had made known his apprehensions of trouble from the disaffected element, warning General Jackson of the dangers possible from this quarter. The Legislature was to convene on the twenty-eighth; and it was intimated that the overture for a surrender might be resolved upon that day. Such a possible action, in the very crisis of battle, could be but an attempt to mar-plot the military plans of the commander-in-chief, and to marshal an enemy in the rear. The information brought in so abruptly on that morning by Colonel Declouet made a profound impression on the mind of General Jackson. The enemy had already opened the battle of the twenty-eighth of December, with the forward movement of his columns and under the heavy fire of his batteries.

In the excitement of the moment, Jackson gave the verbal order to his aid, Captain Duncan, to be delivered at once to Governor Claiborne for immediate execution. This order, as rendered by Captain Duncan, directed the Governor to summarily close the halls of the Legislature, and to place a guard at the doors to prevent a meeting of the body until further orders. Duncan testified that the General put in emphasis the words: "Tell Governor Claiborne to prevent this, and to blow them up if they attempt it!"

The order was executed. The Governor commissioned General J.B. Labitat, of the Louisiana troops, to enforce it; he placed a guard of soldiers at the doors of the building, and forbade entrance to the members on that day. Captain Duncan had put spurs to his horse and started on a lope to the city with the order. On the way he met Colonel Fortier, an aid to the Governor, who consented to promptly deliver the order, permitting Duncan to return. In the proceedings of the committee, Honourable Levi Wells, member of the House of Representatives from Rapides Parish, testified that on the twenty-eighth, under an order of General Jackson, an armed guard was placed at the doors of the legislative halls in the city of New Orleans, which was to hinder the members from assembling—

.... and even to fire on them, should they dare to persist in their design; and that the life of a representative of the people, and a member of the Body, was exposed to the greatest danger; that a sentinel, to hinder him from repairing to his post, presented his bayonet and threatened to run him through with it, unless he retired, adding to this outrage the most insulting tone.

Through the mediation of friendly counsel the views of both the civil and military chiefs were modified. The order was revoked within twenty-four hours, and the guards withdrawn; on the twenty-ninth, the Legislature was permitted to convene. In the conclusion, the committee exonerated Speaker Guichard and other members of the Legislature referred to as under suspicion, and severely censured Colonel Declouet and Captain Duncan as the indiscreet authors of all the trouble. The measures taken by General Jackson and Governor Claiborne were effectual; while the report of the committee was evidently drawn to modify and explain the imputed indiscretions of some of their fellow-members who had been compromised. The procedure did not include all the legislators; for some of these had volunteered their services, shouldered their muskets, and gone to the front of battle.

A feeling of keen resentment toward General Jackson and some officers involved in this affair was nursed long after by these legislators. After peace was assured and hostilities at an end, the Legislature voted a resolution of thanks for valiant services in defence of Louisiana to the officers and soldiers from the States of Kentucky, Tennessee, and Mississippi, with the request to the Governor that he should convey the sense of this resolution in appropriate terms in a letter each to the officers in command of these troops, respectively. The resolution was as follows:

Resolved, That the thanks of the General Assembly be presented, in the name of the State, to our brave brother soldiers from Tennessee, Kentucky, and the Mississippi Territory, and their gallant leaders, Generals Coffee, Carroll, Thomas, Adair, and Colonel Hinds, for the brilliant share they have had in the defence of this country and the happy harmony they have maintained with the inhabitants and militia of the State.

Magloire Guichard
Speaker of the House of Representatives
Fulwar Skipworth
President of Senate
Wm. C. Claiborne
Governor of State
Approved, February 2nd, 1815

The great chieftain could well afford to pass the slight in silence, hailed as he was by the acclamations of the multitude—the deliverer of the country, and the hero of the nation!

A similar resolution of thanks was voted to the officers and troops of Louisiana, who had so patriotically sprung to arms on the invasion of the enemy, and who had so gallantly fought in the several battles of the campaign. In this resolution separate mention was made of each of the officers of the State troops and their several commands, reciting the meritorious services they had rendered, in terms of special praise, making exceptions of certain officers who had incurred the displeasure of some of the honourable legislators.

Under the first resolution, letters were addressed each to Generals Coffee and Carroll, of Tennessee, to Major Hinds, of Mississippi, and to Generals Thomas and Adair, of Kentucky. As these letters are of similar tenor, we quote only the correspondence with General Adair:

New Orleans
February 25th, 1815

Sir: To a soldier who has done his duty in all the conflicts in which his country has been involved, from the War of Independence to the present moment, it must be matter of great exultation to notice the valour and firmness of the children of his old friends; to be convinced that they are the true descendants of the old stock. That the young men of your brigade should have looked up to you in the hour of battle, as their guide and their shield, is only a continuation of that confidence which their fathers had in a chief whose arm had so often, and so successfully, been raised against the foe. The enclosed Resolution of the General Assembly of Louisiana will show you the high sense which is entertained in this State of your services and of those of your brothers in arms. Be towards them the vehicle of our sentiments, and receive for yourself the assurances of my respect and best wishes.

Wm. C. C. Claiborne
Governor of Louisiana
To General John Adair

The response of General Adair:

Governor Wm. C.C. Claiborne

Sir. I have the honour of acknowledging the receipt of Your Excellency's note, inclosing a Resolution of the Legislature of Louisiana, generously awarding the thanks of the State to the militia from her sister States, who aided in the late successful struggle to expel a powerful invading enemy from her shores.

To a proud American, citizen or soldier, the consciousness of having faithfully discharged his duty to his country must ever be his highest and most lasting consolation. But when to this is added the approbation, the gratitude of the wisest, the most respectable part of the community, with whom and under whose eye it has been his fortune to act, it will ever be esteemed, not only the highest reward for his services, but the most powerful incentive to his future good conduct.

Accept, sir, for the Legislature, my warmest acknowledgments for the honourable mention they have made of the corps to which I belong, and for yourself the esteem and respect so justly due from me, for your polite and highly interesting note of communication; and my best wishes for your health and happiness.

John Adair

General Jackson—
Clash With the Court

A member of the Legislature, Mr. Loillier, severely censured the commander-in-chief for continuing New Orleans and vicinity under martial law after the defeat and embarkation of the British army, and for his arbitrary course in sending a body of Creole troops to a remote camp near Baton Rouge, in response to their petition for a discharge. Jackson ordered his arrest. Loillier applied to Judge Hall, of the United States District Court, for a writ of habeas corpus, which was promptly granted by the court. General Jackson summarily ordered the arrest of Judge Hall also; and that he and the assemblyman both be deported beyond the military lines, as persons liable to incite insubordination and mutiny within the martial jurisdiction. Intelligence of the treaty of peace at Ghent soon followed, and martial law once again yielded to civil authority.

Judge Hall, resenting what he deemed a great indignity upon the court, issued an order, summoning Jackson to appear before him to answer a grave charge of contempt. Jackson's attorney attempted to plead in his defence, but the judge silenced him, and set the hearing a week after. On the thirty-first of March, Jackson appeared in court in person, but refused to be interrogated. As his defence had been denied, he announced that he was there only to receive the sentence of the court. Judge Hall then imposed a fine of one thousand dollars, which sum the veteran offender drew from his pocket and handed in to the court.

These proceedings were attended with profound excitement throughout the city and community. The hero of the day had a determined following present in crowds at and near the court-room; and among these were the Baratarian contingent, with their leaders, and others as desperate as these. But the great commander had set the example of implicit obedience to the law, and no disrespect to the court was shown. But as the General sought to retire from the scene, the enthusiasm of the crowds overleaped all bounds of propriety. With shouts and roars of applause the devoted people lifted him in their arms and upon their shoulders, and bore him in triumph through the streets of the city to his headquarters, despite the chagrin and helpless protestations of the victim of their admiration. Tall and gaunt, and angular in person, with his long, spare limbs dangling helplessly about him, and rocked and swayed by the movement of the masses under him, the great warrior was never in all his life before in a position more awkward and undignified. The master of men and emergencies was unthroned for one time in life.

The money to pay the fine was proffered over and over again to reimburse him by ardent friends, but Jackson would listen to no terms of payment of the fine, except out of his own purse. He alone had committed the offense—if there was an offense—and he alone would assume to pay the penalty. It was not until 1844, one year before his death, that Congress passed an act to refund the principal and interest, which amounted then to twenty-seven hundred dollars. In advocacy of this bill Stephen A. Douglas, then Senator from Illinois, made his maiden speech upon the floor of the Senate of the United States.

CHAPTER 33

England and the
Mississippi Valley

There are evidences that the English Government had revived an old dream of conquest and expansion, by which she might once again establish dominion west of the Alleghany Mountains, by the capture of New Orleans, the key to the lower Mississippi Valley. It is a well-known fact in history that that government refused to recognize the legitimacy of the sale and transfer of the Territory of Louisiana by Napoleon to the United States. She had looked upon the transaction with a covetous and jealous eye, for she had nursed the hope some day of adding to her own vast possessions, by conquest or purchase, not only the domain of Louisiana, but that of Florida also. Had it not been that she was engrossed with her military and naval forces in the turbulent wars in Europe, during the ascendant period of Napoleon, the British Government would most probably have employed her armies and navies mainly in the accomplishment of these aims of territorial aggrandizement. Her invasion of the Northwest territory from Canada, at the opening of the War of 1812-15, which so disastrously ended with the destruction of the British fleet by Commodore Perry on Lake Erie, and the annihilation of the British army by General Harrison at the battle of the Thames, was but an entering wedge to her deep designs. After the fall of Napoleon and the pacification of Europe relieved her armies and navies of further service on that side of the ocean, she, in her pride and insolence, believed that she would be invincible in America. Her cherished dream might now at last be realized by the conquest and permanent possession of Louisiana. We have mentioned the significant fact that overtures for peaceful negotiations had been mutually arranged as early as January, 1814, and commissioners soon after appointed to meet at Ghent. When the capitulation at Paris and the exile of Napoleon to Elba occurred within a few brief months, repeated excuses for the delay of negotiations by the British envoys were made. The United States wanted peace on equitable terms, for she had nothing to gain by continuing the war. England dallied and delayed; meanwhile marshalling her military and naval forces for a final crushing blow on her American foe. When articles of peace were signed on the twenty-fourth of December, the British Government knew that information of the event would not reach the belligerents in the Gulf of Mexico until some time in February. But His Majesty, the King of England, and his councillors, confidently believed, as did the officers in command of the English army and navy in this expedition, that the victorious invaders would eat their Christmas dinner in the subjugated city of New Orleans, and there to stay.

Gleig, an educated officer with the army of invasion, who became the chief English historian of the campaign, in his *Narrative*, has to say:

> The primary cause of our defeat may be traced to a source more distant than I have mentioned; I mean to the disclosure of our designs to the enemy. How this occurred, I shall not take upon me to declare; though several rumours bearing at least the guise of probabil-

ity have been circulated. The attack on New Orleans was professedly a secret expedition, so secret indeed that it was not communicated to the inferior officers and soldiers in the armament until immediately previous to our quitting Jamaica. To the Americans, however, it appears to have been long known before. And hence it was that, instead of taking them unawares, we found them fully prepared for our reception. *That our failure is to be lamented no one will deny, since the conquest of New Orleans would have been, beyond all comparison, the most valuable acquisition that could be made to the British dominion throughout the whole Western hemisphere. In possession of that post, we should have kept the entire Southern trade of the United States in check, and furnished means of commerce to our own merchants, of incalculable value.*

On the 29th of August, 1814, Colonel Edward Nichols, in command of the land forces quartered in the Spanish capital of Pensacola, issued a proclamation, from which we quote:

Natives of Louisiana! On you the first call is made to assist in liberating from a faithless, imbecile government, your paternal soil. Spaniards, Frenchmen, Italians, and British; whether settled, or residing for a time in Louisiana, on you also, I call to aid me in this just cause. The American usurpation in this country must be abolished, and the lawful owners of the soil put in possession. I am at the head of a large body of Indians, well armed, disciplined, and commanded by British officers, a good train of artillery with every requisite, seconded by the powerful aid of a numerous squadron of ships. Be assured, your property, your laws, the tranquillity and peace of your country, will be guaranteed to you. Rest assured that these brave

Indians only burn with an ardent desire of satisfaction for the wrongs they have suffered from the Americans, to join you in liberating the southern province from their yoke, and drive them into the limits formerly prescribed by my sovereign. The Indians have pledged themselves not to injure the persons or properties of any but enemies to their Spanish or English fathers. A flag, Spanish, French, or British, over any door, will be a certain protection.

Inhabitants of Kentucky! You have too long borne with grievous impositions. The whole brunt of the war has fallen on your brave sons; be imposed on no longer; but either range yourselves under the standard of your forefathers, or observe a strict neutrality. If you comply, whatever provisions you send down will be paid for in dollars, and the safety of the persons bringing it, as well as the free navigation of the Mississippi, will be guaranteed to you.

Men of Kentucky! Let me call to your minds the conduct of those factions which hurried you into this civil, unjust, and unnatural war, at a time when Great Britain was straining every nerve in defence of her own, and the liberties of the world. Europe is now happy and free, and now hastens justly to avenge an unprovoked insult. Accept of my offers; everything I have promised, I guarantee to you, on the sacred honour of a British officer.

We might repeat such evidences of the purposes and plans of the expedition to Louisiana. But we will close the subject with the impressions of General Jackson himself. In a contribution to the Philadelphia Times, of the 1st of November, 1898, Colonel A.C. Buell, authority for the following says:

It was related to me by the late Governor William Allen, of Ohio, when, as correspondent of the Missouri Republican, I visited the venerable statesman at his home near Chillicothe, in 1875. After an interview on the current political situation, Governor Allen became reminiscent. A scrap-book beats the best of memories in the world; so I will quote from my scrap-book the exact text of this reminiscence. The Governor said:

Shortly after Arkansas was admitted into the Union, in 1836, I, being a member of Congress, then called at the White House. General Jackson—he always preferred to be called General, rather than Mr. President—invited me to lunch with him. No sooner were we seated, than he said: Mr. Allen, let us take a little drink to the new star in the flag;—Arkansas! This ceremony being duly observed, the General continued: Allen, if there had been disaster, instead of victory, at New Orleans, there would never have been a State of Arkansas.

This, of course, interested me; and I asked: Why do you say that, General?

Then he answered that: If Pakenham had taken New Orleans, the British would have claimed and held the whole of Louisiana Purchase.

But, I said, you know, General Jackson, that the Treaty of Ghent, which had been signed fifteen days before the decisive battle, provided for the restoration of all territory, places and possessions, taken by either nation from the other, during the war, with certain unimportant exceptions.

Yes, of course, Jackson replied, but the minutes of the conference at Ghent, as kept by Mr. Gallatin, represent the British commissioners as declaring in exact words: "We do not admit Bonaparte's construction of the law of nations; we can not accept it in relation to any subject-matter before us."

At that moment, pursued General Jackson, none of our commissioners knew what the real meaning of those words was. When they were uttered the British commissioners knew that Pakenham's expedition had been decided on; our commissioners did not know it. Now, since I have been Chief Magistrate, I have learned, from diplomatic sources of the most unquestionable authority, that the British ministry did not intend the Treaty of Ghent to apply to the Louisiana Purchase at all. The whole corporation of them,—Pitt, the Duke of Portland, Grenville, Perceval, Lord Liverpool, and Castlereagh, denied *in toto* the legal right of Napoleon to sell Louisiana to us. They held, therefore, that we had no right to that Territory. So you see, Allen, that the words of Mr. Gouldburn, on behalf of the British commissioners, which I have quoted to you from Albert Gallatin's minutes of the conference, had a far deeper significance than our commissioners could penetrate. These words were meant to lay the foundation for a claim on the Louisiana Purchase, entirely external to the provisions of the Treaty of Ghent. And in that way, the British government was signing a treaty with one hand in front, whilst the other hand, behind its back, was dispatching Pakenham's army to seize the fairest of our possessions.

You can also see, my dear Allen, said the old General, waxing warmer, you can also see what an awful mess such a situation would have been, if the British programme had been carried out in full. But Providence willed otherwise. All the tangled web that the cunning of English diplomacy could weave around our unsuspecting commissioners at Ghent was torn to pieces, and soaked with British blood, in half an hour, at New Orleans, by the never-missing rifles of my Tennessee and Kentucky pioneers; and that ended it. British diplomacy could do wonders; but it could not provide against such a contingency as that. Now, Allen, you have the whole story; and know why Arkansas was saved to the Union.

CHAPTER 34

Just Like Jackson

During the war of 1812-15, the officials of the English Government, civil and military, distinguished themselves by their haughty arrogance and insulting tone of superiority toward the American people; and were, with revengeful malice, guilty of vandalism, spoliations, and cruelties, which were a disgrace to civilization, not to speak of the massacres and butcheries of thousands of women and children by the savage Indians, whom they employed and paid to commit these crimes. Andrew Jackson soon put an end to these English barbarisms wherever he commanded the American armies. An incident, illustrative of his summary methods of dealing with the insolence of his enemies in authority, occurred at Pensacola. The English fleet and army had come in and quartered there in the Spanish capital, with the approval and aid of the Spanish governor, though Spain was at peace with the United States. The British assured him that they would soon be in possession of Louisiana and the coast country, and would fully protect the Spaniard as an ally and friend. When Jackson marched his army to Pensacola, and sent in a message to the governor to expel the British soldiers from the city and order their fleet out of the harbour, the reply of the Spaniard was truckling to the English in tone and evasive and insolent toward the American officer in command. General Jackson replied in the following language:

Your Excellency has been candid enough to admit your having supplied the Indians with arms. In addition to this, I have learned that a British flag has been seen flying on one of your forts. All this is done while you are pretending to be neutral. You can not be surprised then; but on the contrary will provide a fort in your town for my soldiers and Indians, should I take it into my head to pay you a visit. In future, I beg you to withhold your insulting charges against my government, for one more inclined to listen to slander than I am; nor consider me any more as a diplomatic character, unless so proclaimed to you from the mouths of my cannon.

The old hero meant all he said; for he marched upon the town, forced a surrender, sent the British flying to their ships for safety, and compelled the fleet to put to sea.

CHAPTER 35

Humiliation of England

No event in the modern history of her military operations brought a deeper disappointment and a keener sense of humiliation to the English Government, and to the nation, than did the disastrous failure of this expedition, fitted out in haughty pride for the invasion and conquest of Louisiana. The true story of the campaign and battles was in the main suppressed by the Tory press, in the interest of the reigning dynasty and to save the pride and prestige of a really great and imperial people. A coincidence occurred to aid in diverting the mind of the public from the contemplation of the deplorable event. On the 23rd of February, 1815, news of the defeat at New Orleans reached London. On the same day arrived the intelligence of the escape of Napoleon from Elba, and of his landing on the shores of France. Public attention was diverted by the new sensation. The government press fostered the illusion, and the horrors of New Orleans were not so fully known or felt.

William Cobbett, the noted Liberal essayist and author, of England, wrote of the event: "And this was all the people of the duped nation ever heard of the matter. Bonaparte had landed from Elba, and the battle of Waterloo soon succeeded. Both the Government and the people were glad to forget all about this unmerciful beating in America. This battle of New Orleans broke the heart of European despotism. The man who won it did, in that one act, more for the good and the honour of the human race than ever was done by any other man."

The author, discussing the incidents and issues of this remarkable campaign, in the light of the vast superiority in both military and naval forces of the British over the Americans, their more thorough equipment, and their veteran discipline under the best-trained officers in the world, put the inquiry: "How can we account for the repeated reverses, and the final over-whelming defeat and expulsion from the country, of such a vast and formidable armament by an inferior body of raw recruits, suddenly improvised for defence from the militia of the country, and but poorly armed and equipped?" "Providence!" was the reply; nothing less than Providence could have baffled and beaten such a powerful foe, bent on conquest and spoliation for a wicked purpose, with a wicked spirit, and in a wicked cause. England's boastful pride and intolerant and cruel insolence toward her American kindred was humbled at last. The God of battle had once again in time punished a strong nation for its stubborn crimes, and given victory to the oppressed. Providence was with Jackson and his militia!

CHAPTER 36

Death of Lord Pakenham

Pakenham died the death of the brave soldier, the heroic Briton, and the beloved commander. His wounds were mortal, and he was at once borne back to headquarters unconscious and dying. No last words came down to us through the grief-stricken aids who ministered to him in his last hour. The British accounts of his wounding and death-scenes are conflicting and unsatisfactory. Judge Walker, in his work, "Jackson and New Orleans," after much research, says that Pakenham was wounded first while attempting to rally the Forty-fourth Regiment, whose chief officer, Colonel Mullins, had failed to lead it to a second attack, after the first repulse by the Tennessee and Kentucky infantry. A musket-ball broke his right arm, and another killed his horse. His aid, Captain McDougall, assisted him to mount his own horse, a Creole pony, and led him forward by the bridle-rein, the General's wounded arm hanging helpless at his side. Pakenham continued in front, and to encourage his men. As the Ninety-third Highlanders came up, he raised his hat in his left hand, waved it in the air with enthusiasm, and shouted:

"Hurrah! Hurrah! brave Highlanders!"

A discharge of grape-shot almost annihilated the group. One shot passed through the General's thigh, and at the same time through the body of the pony, and both went down, never to rise again. As the aid raised him once again in his arms, the chief received a third and fatal wound in the groin. He was borne back then, near to his headquarters, and placed under a large oak tree, where, beyond the surgeon's skill, he shortly breathed his last.

From English authorities we learn that there were in the English army, under Pakenham, regiments that had won laurels at Martinique, Badajoz, Salamanca, Vittoria, the Pyrenees, and Toulouse. The English chronicler, Cooke, says of some of these veterans, who touched, on their way to America from the coasts of France, the shore of Old England for a few days, that "scraps from our colours, or other little souvenirs, were craved for with outstretched hands, to find a resting place in the fair bosoms of the ladies of Devonshire."

Others again were but recently transported from the fiery ordeals of Corunna, Busaco, and Ciudad Rodrigo, says the same author. England never sent forth from her borders a braver or better-disciplined body of soldiers, as was proven in every trial of campaign and battle of the invasion of Louisiana. No other troops in the world could have behaved with more sturdy gallantry or fought with superior courage.

CHAPTER 37

Personalities

General Andrew Jackson

Andrew Jackson was born in the Waxhaw settlement on the 15th of March, 1767, so near the border of North and South Carolina as to leave it a question of contention as to which State may claim the honour of his nativity. His father, Andrew Jackson, came over from Carrickfergus, on the north coast of Ireland, in 1765. His mother was Elizabeth Hutchinson. The father died before the birth of Andrew. His birthplace was a rude log cabin of the border. His education was limited to the elementary studies of the country schools of his day. At the age of fourteen he entered the colonial army, and, young as he was, displayed the same spirit of patriotic courage and indomitable will that made him famous. Two elder brothers had entered the army before him, and both gave their lives a sacrifice to the cause of liberty. The mother died soon, of grief and the hardships of war. Young Andrew was taken prisoner, and roughly treated by his captors. He was nearly starved in prison at Camden. While thus confined, an English officer insolently ordered him one day to black his boots. Jackson indignantly refused, for which offense the brutal officer beat him over his head with his sword, inflicting injuries which caused suffering in after life. This incident is related to have greatly intensified

Jackson's hatred of the English throughout his life. An orphan, and alone in the world, when the War of the Revolution was over he was apprenticed to learn the saddler's trade. At eighteen he began the study of law, in the office of McCoy, in Salisbury.

In 1788, Jackson was appointed public prosecutor for western North Carolina, now Tennessee. He removed and located at Nashville, and very soon was engaged in an active and remunerative practice. In 1796, he sat as a delegate in the convention at Knoxville, to frame a constitution for Tennessee, admitted into the Union as a State in that year. He was the first representative in Congress of the new State. But one year afterward, he was elected a senator of the United States Congress. In 1798, he resigned his seat in the Senate to accept an appointment as judge of the Supreme Court of his State, which office he held for six years. He engaged repeatedly in personal rencounters and duels, and in the latter received wounds that caused him great physical suffering during life.

Since 1801, he had been commander of the Tennessee militia. On the declaration of war against England, Jackson offered his services, with twenty-five hundred troops, to the Government for the defence of the country. He was ordered to Natchez with two thousand men to operate against any movement of the enemy on New Orleans. No enemy appearing on the coast, he was ordered by Secretary Armstrong, of the War Department, to disband his army. This foolish order Jackson disobeyed, and very properly led his men back to Tennessee before dismissing them. His famous campaign against the great Creek nation, in 1814, and his repeated victories over these savage allies of England, breaking their power and compelling peace; his Gulf Coast campaign and battles around New Orleans, crushing the British army and driving it from the country; his successful career as President of the United States, are well known in the history of our nation, and distinguish him as one of the ablest and most forceful characters our country has ever produced. He died at the Hermitage, full of honours and renown, on the 8th of June, 1845, having lived a patriot citizen, an able military chieftain, and a great leader in the civic affairs of State and nation.

ISAAC SHELBY, GOVERNOR OF KENTUCKY

Fortunate was it for Kentucky and for the nation that Isaac Shelby directed the military affairs of the Commonwealth during the period of the second war with England. This famous pioneer of the famous pioneers of Kentucky was born in Maryland, on the 11th of December, 1750, near Hagerstown. Early in life he was employed as a land surveyor. On the threatened invasion of Virginia by the federated army of the Northwest tribes under the celebrated chief, Cornstalk, he was lieutenant of a company in the command of his father, General Evan Shelby, and gained distinction for gallant services in the great victory won at Point Pleasant on the 10th of October, 1774, which forced the Indians to sue for peace. He visited Kentucky in 1775, with the vanguard of pioneer explorers, and marked the lands which afterward, in 1780, he returned and secured by entry and upon which he settled with his family after the Revolutionary War.

When he removed from Maryland, he settled near the borderline of Virginia and North Carolina, then not well defined. Believing his residence on Virginia soil, he was elected to the Virginia Legislature in 1779. But the survey of the boundary line determined him a citizen of North Carolina, and as such he was officially known after until his final removal to Kentucky. In the gloomiest period of the

Isaac Shelby, Governor of Kentucky

War for Independence, in the southern colonies, after the defeat at Camden and the surrender of Charleston, Shelby became famous as a border leader of what seemed the forlorn hope of the colonists, and for his frequent victories over the enemy. With Colonels Sevier and Clarke, he led his command to the attack and capture of a strong fort in the Cherokee country, which had, garrisoned by British, Tories, and Indians, greatly harassed the settlers in west North Carolina. Soon after, in August, 1780, he inflicted a loss of several hundred by an attack on the British at Musgrove's Mill, South Carolina, and escaped with little loss of his own men. But his greatest victory, and one of the most decisive of the war, was won at King's Mountain. Joining forces with Colonels Sevier and Campbell, a bold attack was planned and made on the notorious General Ferguson, encamped on King's Mountain. Without artillery, these frontiersmen, with their flint-lock rifles, boldly attacked Ferguson's veterans, advancing on the enemy up the mountain side, and keeping up the fight until Ferguson and nearly four hundred of his men were slain, and over seven hundred made prisoners.

After the close of the war, in the winter of 1782-3, General Shelby removed to Kentucky and settled in Lincoln County, where he remained through life at his elegant home and upon his ample estate, the model citizen and patriot. His civic and military fame preceded him, for many of his soldiers of the Revolution were his emigrant neighbours. When Kentucky took the initial steps toward Statehood in the Union, Shelby was a member of the convention of 1787-8, and also of the convention to frame the first constitution, of 1792. By unanimous consent, he became the first Governor of the Commonwealth, in 1792, and was inaugurated as Governor at Lexington on the first of June. On the sixth of June, in courtly style, the Governor appeared in person in presence of the legislators, in joint assembly, and read to the august body his first message, formally delivering to the Speakers of each House a copy in manuscript, and then retired in dignified state, when the Speakers each adjourned the members to their respective halls. This was in imitation of the custom of the British monarchs, followed by the colonial governors in America, and by Washington himself in his first inaugural ceremonies.

So much had Governor Shelby established himself in the esteem and confidence of the people, that with unanimity he was elected a second time to serve as Governor in the critical period of 1812, when a second war with England became a certainty. His indomitable and patriotic zeal counted no costs and reckoned at no sacrifice to punish the invaders and drive them from our soil during the three years of hostilities. In this time, under his several calls, over twenty thousand volunteers were sent to the Army of the Northwest under Harrison, from Kentucky. By these mainly, the shameful surrender of Hull, at Detroit, was retrieved, the victory of the Thames won, and the British and their Indian allies driven from the borders, from Detroit to Buffalo, for the remainder of the war. At the battle of the Thames, won by Kentuckians, Governor Shelby led the three thousand volunteers whom he had called out for this campaign, in person, though in his sixty-fourth year of age. On his return to the capital of his State, when a last requisition was made by the Secretary of War, in 1814, thousands of volunteers answered his call for troops to reinforce the army of General Jackson in the Southwest, of whom three regiments, of twenty-two hundred men, were accepted and sent to New Orleans. Governor Shelby notified the Government at Washington that, if ten thousand soldiers were needed to repel the enemy and drive him from our soil in the Southwest, Kentucky was ready to supply them on brief notice.

Peace once again reigned when his second term as Governor ended. He retired to his country home, where he spent the evening of his life, honoured and esteemed by a grateful and devoted constituency of citizenship as few men were. He died at his home on the 26th of July, 1826, in the ripeness of years and of honours.

General John Adair

John Adair was born in Chester County, S.C., in 1759, and was the son of Baron William Adair, of Scotland, whose wife was a Moore. After remaining some years in South Carolina, Baron Adair returned to Scotland. The son became a soldier in the Revolutionary War when quite a youth, and served with gallantry in the colonial army. He was made prisoner, and was treated with repeated cruelties by the enemy. He was a member of the convention which ratified the Constitution of the United States. He removed to Kentucky in 1787, and settled in Mercer County. He took an active and prominent part in the Indian border wars, having been appointed major by General Wilkinson. He was in many frays with the savages, in one of which, after several repulses of a body of Indians largely outnumbering his own forces, he was defeated by Chief Little Turtle, though he brought off his men after inflicting more serious losses on the enemy than his own. This was near Fort St. Clair, in Ohio. In 1793, General Scott appointed him a lieutenant-Colonel. He represented Mercer County in the Legislature several times, and was once Speaker of the House.

Adair's name became involved with Aaron Burr's in the military movements in Kentucky and the Southwest which have become known in history as "Burr's Conspiracy," as did the names of Andrew Jackson and other prominent men of this country, of unquestioned loyalty to our nation.

Burr's designs, with all the lights thrown upon the question, have remained a mystery to this day. If he contemplated ultimate treason, he did not fully disclose it to many who were disposed to sympathize with and to lend aid to what they were persuaded was a legitimate expedition to wrest from Spanish rule territory in dispute, or which "manifest destiny" determined should come under the rule of the United States as against the aggressions of Spain or England. Burr undoubtedly misled many good and patriotic men, who abandoned his fortunes when the intimations of treasonable designs were charged against him, which brought him to trial.

In 1805, when John Breckinridge resigned his seat in the United States Senate to become attorney-general under Jefferson, Adair was elected to fill the unexpired term. He entered the military service again, and at the battle of Thames River acted as volunteer aid to Governor Shelby. For gallant conduct on this occasion he was made a brigadier-general in 1814. He took a leading part in recruiting the volunteer troops for the reinforcement of Jackson's army at New Orleans, and in their transportation down the river. General Thomas. in chief command of these, being prostrated with illness, the command fell upon General Adair. He displayed courage and military skill in the disposition of his troops, and especially in the final contest on the eighth of January, under difficulties that were seriously embarrassing.

In 1820, he was elected governor of Kentucky, and held this office when the great questions of relief, and Old Court and New Court, began to disturb the peace and tranquillity of the Commonwealth. In 1831, he was elected a member of Congress, and in the national house served on the Committee on Military Affairs. He died on the 19th of May, 1840, and was buried in the State cemetery at Frankfort, where a monument, erected at the cost of the State, with proper inscription, stands over his grave. A fine oil portrait of him hangs on the wall of the capitol, at Frankfort.

Colonel Gabriel Slaughter

Who commanded a regiment of Kentucky troops in the battle of New Orleans, was a native of Virginia, but immigrated to Kentucky in pioneer days and settled in Mercer County, about four miles east of Harrodsburg, on the turnpike road leading to Lexington. Though a man of ability, and much esteemed, he seems to have lived in the retirement of private life until the maturity of middle age. He early became a member of the Baptist church, in which he led a consistent and zealous life, taking a prominent part as a layman in the promotion of the interests of religion and of the denomination with whom he fraternized. His character and worth made him prominent among the brotherhood. He often represented his church as its messenger, and was usually called to preside as moderator over the associations within the jurisdictions of which he lived. His hospitality was of that warm and generous kind which was characteristic of pioneer days. His ample and comfortable country mansion, situated upon a much-frequented highway, came to be known far and wide as the "Wayfarer's Rest."

Under the call of Governor Shelby, in 1814, he enlisted a regiment of volunteers for the army of the Southwest from Mercer County and the counties adjacent, which was one of three regiments accepted for this service. The gallant and distinguished part taken at New Orleans, in the great battle of the eighth of January, by Colonel Slaughter and his regiment, has been set forth in the pages of this book. No troops engaged on the American side on that day did more

GABRIEL SLAUGHTER, 11TH GOVERNOR OF KENTUCKY

fatal execution upon the enemy's rank and file than did these. Every man of the regiment was in rifle-range, and all did deadly work.

Though courteous and gentle in manner, Colonel Slaughter was possessed of invincible firmness and independence when occasion required or a sense of duty urged. An incident illustrates. General Jackson, who held him in high esteem, appointed him to preside over a court-martial. The decision did not meet with the favour of the chief, and he ordered a reconsideration and reversal of proceedings. Colonel Slaughter declined to comply, saying: "I know my duty, and have performed it." Jackson's esteem was not lessened by the manliness of the answer.

His gallantry at New Orleans brought the name of Colonel Slaughter prominently to political notice, and the next year, 1816, he was nominated and elected lieutenant-governor, on the ticket with George Madison for governor. Madison was not destined to wear the civic honours which an ardent constituency had woven to crown him. He died in October, a few months after the election. Slaughter succeeded him, and was duly installed as governor. An active opposition party made an open issue of the question as to whether the lieutenant-governor was eligible to become governor by succession, under the Constitution, or that a successor should be chosen at an election to be called by act of the Legislature. There had been no precedent to this date. The question was fiercely agitated, in and out of the legislative halls, during two years of the executive term, before a subsidence of partisan feeling ended the contest. Governor Slaughter held firmly to his convictions of constitutional right, came safely through the angry waves of opposition, and served out his term of four years with credit to himself and the Commonwealth. The question was settled by this precedent, no more to be raised, that, under the constitutional provisions then in force, the lieutenant-governor should succeed to the office of governor upon the "death, resignation, or refusal to qualify" of the governor-elect.

On the expiration of his term Governor Slaughter retired to his country home, and resumed his occupation as a farmer, leading a quiet and useful citizen life until the end. He died at his home in 1830, aged sixty-three years.

CHAPTER 38

Kentucky's Contribution to the War of 1812-15

It is worthy of mention to the credit of Kentucky that, with a population of four hundred thousand, she furnished for the nation's defence, during the three years of war with England and the savages who allied with her, forty regiments of volunteer militia, besides a number of battalions and companies, over twenty-four thousand men in all, from 1812 to 1815. Excepting a small force of volunteers from the then Territory of Ohio, and a few regulars, her troops made up the entire body of the army of General Harrison in the Northwest campaign, ending with the decisive and crushing victory at the battle of Thames River, over the combined army of British under General Proctor, and Indians under Tecumseh. That battle was fought and won by the impetuous charges of the Kentuckians, under Colonel Richard M. Johnson, against the Indians, and his brother, Colonel James Johnson, against the British, before the forces in the rear, mainly Kentuckians also, could be brought into action. Before Commodore Perry met the English fleet on Lake Erie, he called for one hundred riflemen from Harrison's army to perch upon the masts and rigging of his ships, as sharpshooters, to pick off the seamen and gunners from the enemy's decks. One hundred Kentuckians volunteered in this perilous service, and others vied with them the honours of the place, though all were landsmen and strangers to the sea. The British commodore made a similar call on Proctor's men and Tecumseh's Indians, but none cared to confront the dangers of such a service. The fleets coming to close quarters, the deadly fire of the riflemen in the rigging helped to strew the decks of the enemy's ships with dead and wounded, and to silence the guns by shooting down the gunners.

Appendices

LIST OF KENTUCKIANS IN THE BATTLE OF NEW ORLEANS

I

ROLL OF FIELD AND STAFF, MITCHUSSON'S REGIMENT OF KENTUCKY DETACHED MILITIA, WAR OF 1812, COMMANDED BY LIEUTENANT-COLONEL WILLIAM MITCHUSSON

WILLIAM MITCHUSSON, Lieut.-colonel
SAMUEL PARKER, Lieutenant-colonel.
REUBEN HARRISON, Major.
THOMPSON CRENSHAW, Major.
JOSIAH RAMSEY, Adjutant.
CHRISTOPHER G. HONTS, Quartermaster.

WILLIAM PRINCE, Paymaster.
JOHN C. PENTECOST, Surgeon.
STEPHEN C. DORRIS, Surgeon's Mate.
ISAAC CALDWELL, Sergeant-major.
MOSES THOMPSON, Quartermaster-sergt.
JOHNSON LOUGHLIN, Fife Major.

CAPTAIN THOMAS GRIFFIN'S COMPANY

THOMAS GRIFFIN, Captain.
BOSWELL PULLIAM, Lieutenant.
ALLEN HAYS, Ensign.
DAVENPORT VENABLE, Sergeant.
TERENCE KIRBY, Sergeant.
SIMEON ACTON, Sergeant.
SAMUEL SPILMAN, Sergeant.

WILLIAM BAIRD, Corporal.
JOHN O'NEAL, Corporal.
JONATHAN EWBANK, Corporal.
ALEXANDER CHAMBERS, Corporal.
JAMES C. PULLIAM, Drummer.
JOSEPH RIGHT, Fifer.

PRIVATES

Brown, James,
Baird, David,
Bigsby, John,
Biggs, David,
Berry, John,
Button, John,
Button, Zacheus,
Bardwell, James,
Bass, Isaac,
Creek, David,
Chayson, David,
Cowin, James,
Cowen, John.

Dobson, Thomas,
Dry, John,
Deal, Henry,
Doke, William,
Dowell, David,
Emberton, John,
Fraley, Nicholas,
Garrett, Joseph,
Grisane, Samuel,
Gibson, John,
Gressom, Thomas,
Hobach, Mark,
Highsmith, William,

Horton, Daniel,
Hamilton, Robert,
Hoofman, Elam,
Huckaboy, Joseph,
Huckaboy, Nathan,
James, Jacob,
Jackson, Elijah,
Johnson, Luther,
Johnson, Robert,
Kirby, John,
Kirby, Leonard,
Kirby, Isaiah,
Lee, Mathias,

Miller, Samuel,
Morris, Miles,
Meadows, Jesse,
Noles, Robert,
Nelson, William,
Oliver, Dury,
Pruett, Moses,
Pinkerton, James,
Rigsby, John,

Ragland, Benjamin,
Sayres, John,
Stovall, Dury,
Seagrave, John,
Springer, John,
Slaton, Ezekiel,
Stamp, Charles,
Thompson, John,

Wetherspoon, James,
Williams, Milam,
Weatherspoon, Wiley,
Welch, Thomas,
Weatherspoon, Major,
Wooten, Daniel,
Wiley, John,
Wildman, Burnell.

CAPTAIN ROBERT SMITH'S COMPANY

ROBERT SMITH, Captain.
MORTON A. RUCKER, Lieutenant.
ASA TURNER, Ensign.
THOMAS KILGORE, Sergeant.
PETER CASH, Sergeant.
DANIEL POWELL, Sergeaut.
JOHN PETERS, Sergeant.

WILLIAM SANDEFEW, Sergeant.
CHRISTOPHER HARDESTY, Corporal.
CHARLES W. BROWN, Corporal.
JAMES MILLER, Corporal.
JAMES BRUNTS, Corporal.
SAMUEL SKINNER, Drummer.

PRIVATES

Arnet, William,
Butler, Samuel,
Barnes, John,
Bramley, Daniel,
Capps, Joshua,
Crabtree, John F.,
Clements, John,
Crabtree, James,
Calender, Isaac,
Cross, Joseph,
Ducate, James,
Dixon, Payne,
Ezell, Harrison,
Fickas, John,
Fugudy, Benjamin,

Gillum, William H.,
Gibson, John,
Hawthorn, Robert,
Holifield, William,
Hardin, Ennis,
Hardesty, Clemons,
Hendrix, Thomas,
Keatch, Ovid,
Lambert, Joel,
Lambert, William,
Mayo, John,
Martin, Daniel,
Miller, William,
McNamer, Philip,
McGraw, John,

McCoy, James,
Pullom, John,
Parrick, Thomas,
Rolls, Abijah,
Read, James R.,
Stephens, George,
Smith, Matthew,
Skillett, Thomas,
Sutherland, Ransom,
Scott, James W.,
Stephens, Jesse,
Tarpin, William,
Weathers, John,
Wiggins, Joshua.

CAPTAIN THOMAS STERRETT'S COMPANY

THOMAS STERRETT, Captain.
JOHN AUSTIN, Lieutenant.
HENRY HINES, Ensign.
JOHN BREWER, Sergeant.
NATHAN YOUNG, Sergeant.
JAMES B. REVILL, Sergeant.
NICHOLAS KING, Sergeant.

DAVID C. FEELDING, Sergeant.
THOMAS BRIDGES, Corporal.
NATHAN JOHNSON, Corporal.
STEPHEN WADE, Corporal.
JOHN COSTILOW, Drummer.
BENJAMIN TEMPLER, Fifer.

PRIVATE

Bratton, George,
Brown, Henry,
Condra, William,
Carter, William,
Coal, Joseph,
Calvert, John,
Cunningham, Brackett C.,
Dawson, James,
Dawson, Jonas,
Dawson, John,
Dawson, Johnson,
Davis, Thomas,
Evans, Richard,
Ethell, James,
Forkner, Martin,
Fegert, Alexander,
Franklin, Stephen,
Galloway, William,
Hay, James S.,
Heavener, John,
Hammond, Thomas,

Harris, Elijah,
Hendrick, James,
Holloway, Thomas,
Harlan, George,
Jenkins, Samuel,
Johnson, Richard,
Kown, William,
Kown, Nathan,
Kimble, William S.,
Kidwell, James,
Kelsey David,
Lawrence, James H.,
Long, Abner,
Marshall, James,
Mannon, Thomas,
Moge, Jacob,
McClammon, James W.,
McClammon, John S.,
Miller, Philip,
Mannen, William,
McMurry, William,

Newman, Jacob,
Newman, William,
Owensby, Nicholas,
Pollard, Elijah,
Paulk, Moses,
Pitman, William,
Roundtree, Turner,
Roundtree, Kelly B.,
Srader, John,
Stroude, Doran,
Stagner, Jeremiah,
Summons, George,
Stone, John,
Stroud, John,
Templer, Jesse,
Thompson, Edward,
Wilkinson, James,
Wood, Mark D.,
Wood, William,
Wiley, Elijah,
Whitlow, Henry.

CAPTAIN SAMUEL F. MALONE'S COMPANY

SAMUEL F. MALONE, Captain.
ELIAS BUTTON, Lieutenant.
DENNIS COCHRAN, Ensign.
MATTHEW SIMON, Sergeant.
CORNELIUS MANLEY, Sergeant.
JAMES McALISTER, Sergeant.
ROBERT T. ANDERSON, Sergeant.

ABNER WELLS, Corporal.
HEZEKIAH LARD, Corporal.
JAMES GASH, Corporal.
JAMES BLACK, Corporal.
JESSE PULLIAM, Drummer.
JAMES ROBERTSON, Fifer.

PRIVATES

Alexander, Thomas,
Brown, William,
Berry, Moses,
Blair, Andrew,
Bagman, James,
Bloyd, John,
Clark, Roderick,
Clark, Joseph,
Chapman, Job,
Dishmore, James,

Dishmore, William,
Duff, Fielding,
Denison, Zade,
Dewessa, Elisha,
Dunagan, Thomas,
Emerson, William,
Edgar, Josiah,
Edgar, Johnson,
Ellis, Hercules,
Farley Clay,

Greathouse, Hiram,
Garrison, David,
Harris, John L.,
Huffman, Cornelius,
Howell, Hudson,
Handy, Jesse,
Hardin, Thomas,
Hoge, Edmund,
Johnson, John,
Jenkins, William,

Lewis, Charles,
Lyon, William,
Logsdon, John,
Merritt, John,
McKinney, Charles W.,
Mitchell, James,
Newell, John,
Nunegard, William.
Nation, Laban,

O'Neal, Bennett,
Owens, William,
Pickett, John,
Pulliam, John,
Penick, James,
Roundtree, Henry,
Reed, William,
Scott, Robert,
Sutterfield, Eli,

Scott, Joseph,
Tribhle, Harris,
Thacker, Allen,
Taylor, James,
Taylor, Isaac,
Williams, William,
Wheeler, Bond,
Young, Asa.

CAPTAIN JOHN C. DODD'S COMPANY

JOHN C. DODD, Captain.
WILLIAM HARRALL, Lieutenant.
BERT MOORE, Ensign.
ROGER FILLEY, Sergeant.
JORDAN McVAY, Sergeant.
HIRAM PRUNELL, Sergeant.
WILLIAM PERKINS, Sergeant.

WILLIAM STORY, Sergeant.
BENJAMIN D. CERBY, Corporal.
MAHALA INGRAM, Corporal.
JOHN SULLIVAN, Corporal.
ROBERT RICHEY, Corporal.
FLEMING CASTLEBERG, Drummer.
WILLIAM LAUGHLIN, Fifer.

PRIVATES

Anderson, Evan,
Baker, Seth,
Barnett, Samuel,
Bridges, Thomas,
Bridges, William,
Barton, William,
Bird, Jacob,
Cammack, William,
Carlew, Henry,
Campbell, Lindsey,
Carter, James,
Carlew, John,
Cannon, Israel,
Carlew, Robert,
Davidson, Alexander B.,
Dison, Bennett,
Drennan, Samuel,
Dunn, Alexander,
Duff, James,
Entricon, John,
French, Joseph,
Green, Levi,
Gaskins, Thadeus,
Green, James,

Gilkey, John,
George, Pallam,
Hancock, John,
Hughes, James,
Heath, Riland,
Hobart, Joseph,
Jenkins, Arthur B.,
Jenkins, Whitenell W.,
Kenady, William,
Long, William,
Leech, Abner,
Lamb, William,
Leech, Zadock,
Law, Samuel,
Love, William,
McNabb, John W.,
Miller, John,
Moore, Edmund,
Mercer, Drury,
McClear, William,
McElhana, William,
Manas, John,
Neily, John,

Nowlin, John,
Pickering, William,
Patterson, Thomas,
Philips, Samuel S.,
Quarles, Stores,
Robison, Kinsey,
Robison, William,
Ritchey, Alexander,
Ramage, Benjamin,
Rhinhart, Samuel,
Robison, Hugh,
Strawmut, John,
Strawmatt, William,
Saxon, Lewis,
Smith, Stephen,
Stations, Moses,
Trimm, Charles,
Taylor, Solomon,
Whitenell, John,
Wadlington, James,
Wells, Henry,
Witherow, Samuel,
Washington, Thomas C.

190

CAPTAIN EDWARD WILBURN'S COMPANY

EDWARD WILBURN, Captain.
JOHN M. CABINESS, Lieutenant.
JAMES BARRING, Ensign.
CHARLES LEWIS, Sergeant.
CHARLES LONG, Sergeant.
HOPKINS BOND, Sergeant.

JAMES WHITE, Sergeant.
JAMES YOUNG, Corporal.
JOHN WILLIAMS, Corporal.
WILLIAM BRISTOE, Corporal.
JOSEPH HOOPER, Corporal.
ANDREW TURPIN, Drummer.

PRIVATES

Anderson, James,
Ashlook, Thomas,
Agee, William,
Allen, Samuel,
Bedford, John C.,
Bunch, Israel,
Banning, Clark,
Burges, John,
Belk, John,
Belk, James,
Craft, Gilbert,
Cheetham, Hezekiah,
Carpenter, James,
Craft, George,
Condrey, Elifus,
Dohirty, Alexander,
Eldridge, William,

French, John,
Gwinn, Joseph,
Hicks, Richard,
Helms, James,
Hollett Solomon,
Jackman, Richard,
Linsey, Henry,
Lynn, James,
Loller, James,
Lynn, Charles,
Lewis, John,
Mitchell, William,
Moody, John,
Murry, John,
Minst, Francis,
McElvain, Samuel,
Nell, Philip,

Newman, Isaac,
Ogden, David,
Reynolds, Charles,
Richardson, Shaderick,
Reynolds, Amos,
Rush, Samuel,
Staton, Joseph,
Stockton, Jesse,
Thurman, William,
Thurman, Littleberry,
Tooly, William,
Vann, John,
Venable, Daniel,
Wilburn, William,
Winfrey, William,
Young, Robert.

CAPTAIN ROBERT PAXTON'S COMPANY

ROBERT PAXTON, Captain.
DANIEL ZIBB, Lieutenant.
WILLIAM RHEA, Ensign.
WILLIAM P. MONTGOMERY, Sergeant.
CAMPBELL GILMORE, Sergeant.
ISHAM READY, Sergeant.
ALEXANDER BROWNLEE, Sergeant.

JAMES ARMES, Sergeant.
ARCHIBALD RHEA, Corporal.
ASHBY JONES, Corporal.
WILLIAM HOGAN, Corporal.
ANTHONY DAVIS, Corporal.
ALLEN MILLER, Rt. W. M.

PRIVATES

Atwell, Richard,
Berry, Franklin,
Butler, Nathan,
Buckingham, Peter,
Baker, William,

Barrett, Thompson,
Broner, William,
Byes, Armstrong,
Batron Robert,
Calhoun, John,

Cunningham, James,
Caldwell, Andrew,
Duncan, James,
Dobson, Joseph,
Dobson, Robert,

191

Faris, John,
Gillingham, John,
Gooch, William,
Good, William,
Hampton, Stephen,
Harvey, John,
Hays, Campbell,
Hays, James I.,
Hays, Andrew E.,
Hunt, James,
Hayes, James,
Hogan, Nathan,
Helton, Thomas,
Hogan, John,
Isaacs, Samuel,
Janes, Berry,
Lampton, Jesse,
Lumpkin, Abraham,

Lisle, Peter,
Lile, Vincent,
Lemons, Isaac,
Montgomery, Robert M.,
Morr, William,
Montgomery, Cyrus,
Moseby, Micajah,
McDaniel, William,
McKinsley, William,
Mathews, Samuel,
McMillan, Joseph M.,
Morris, John,
Ormes, Elly, jr.,
Ormes, Nathan,
Ormes, Elly,
Ormes, Nathan,
Price, Robert,

Riley, William,
Russell, Joseph,
Ray, John,
Raffity, John,
Smith, Isaac,
Skaggs, Charles,
Smith, Thomas,
Smith, Samuel,
Stearman, William,
Tribble, Absalom,
White, John D.,
Waggoner, Willis,
White, John C.,
Wilson, Thomas,
Woodard, Abraham,
White, John,
Wheeler, Charles.

CAPTAIN JAMES ROBISON'S COMPANY

JAMES ROBISON, Captain.
LUKE NICHOLAS, Lieutenant.
GEORGE NEGLEY, Ensign.
THOMAS ARMSTRONG, Sergeant.
LILY SULLIVAN, Sergeant.
SAMUEL ELISON, Sergeant.
JAMES ALEXANDER, Sergeant.

KARR HICKS, Sergeant.
DUNCAN CAMPBELL, Corporal.
EDWARD ROBISON, Corporal.
AARON STALLINGS, Corporal.
ROBERT WILLIAMS, Corporal.
GEORGE LACEY, Fifer.

PRIVATES

Alexander, John,
Aainsworth, Joseph,
Baker, Thomas,
Britt, Robert,
Barnes, Thomas B.,
Byle, John H.,
Blakeley, Samuel,
Boreland, Samuel,
Coleran, Alexander,
Coleman, Robert M.,
Cravins, Jesse,
Dunn, Richard,
Dinsmore, Jacob,
Davis, Clem,
Davis, Joseph,
Darneal, Thomas,

Edwards, Edward,
Furguson, William,
Filson, Jesse,
George, James,
Gare, Isaac,
Gibson, Meredith,
Grace, Henry,
Hamby, James,
Hunter, David,
Hunter, William,
Henderson, Ezekiel,
• Handy, Benjamin,
Hardin, Samuel,
Hardin, Benjamin,
Inman, Thomas,
Lancaster, Henry,

Messick, George,
Morris, Ely,
Messimore, George,
Malin, Thomas,
Mitchell, William,
Mesamore, Jacob,
Nickson, William,
Pyle, William,
Pyle, David,
Stutt, Nicholas,
Shelton, Elijah,
Shelton, William,
Shelton, Abraham,
Savage, William M.,
Shelton, Joseph,
Shelton, Robert,

Smith, Samuel,
Smith, Cloud,
Sullivan, Levi,
Thompson, Lawson,

Thompson, John,
Threet, James,
Thradford, Walker,

Thomas, James,
Tell, Joseph,
Wingard, David.

CAPTAIN ALMY McLEAN'S COMPANY

ALMY McLEAN, Captain.
EPHRAIM M. BRANK, Lieutenant.
WILLIAM ALEXANDER, Lieutenant.
ISAAC DAVIS, Ensign.
JOHN STILL, Sergeant.
HENRY NUSELL, Sergeant.
ENOCH METCALF, Sergeant.

JORDAN O'BRIEN, Sergeant.
JAMES LANGLEY, Corporal.
MOSES MATTHEWS, Corporal.
EDWARD H. TARRANTS, Corporal.
GEORGE HILL, Corporal.
ABNER B. C. DILLINGHAM, Fifer.

PRIVATES

Apling, Henry,
Anderson, John, jr.,
Allen, Linsey,
Anderson, John,
Allison, McLean,
Bishop, James,
Barker, Samuel,
Bone, Cornelius,
Bonds, Lott,
Carter, James,
Craig, John,
Combs, Jesse,
Cob, Elijah,
Craig, Robert,
Crouch, Isaac,
Claxton, Jeremiah,
Dewitt, William,
Donnald, James,
Evans, James,
Ferguson, John K.,
Foley, Mason,
Fox, Nathan,

Fowler, Jeremiah,
Gany, Matthew,
Gant, Thomas,
Gamblin, John,
Grayham, William,
Hewlett, Thomas,
Hines John,
Howard, Isaac,
Hensley, Leftridge,
Hewlett, Lemuel,
Hubbard, Liner,
Jains, Edward,
Kern, George,
Kennedy, George F.,
Lott, James,
Lynn, Gasham,
Lynn, Henry,
Leece, Samuel,
McGill, James,
Moore, Thomas,
Matthews, Jacob,
McFerson, James,

Martin, John,
Macons, Peter,
Nanny, Spencer,
Norris, Thomas,
Nixon, James,
Penrod, George,
Ripple, Michael,
Row, Adam,
Ripple, Jacob,
Rhodes, Bradford,
Sever, Michael,
Sumner, Thomas,
Sumner, William,
Sunn, John F.,
Sanders, George,
Voris, John,
Wilcox, Elias,
Williams, Noah,
Wade, Hendley,
Wilson, John,
Williams, William,
Yaunce, Lawrence.

CAPTAIN ROBERT PATTERSON'S COMPANY

ROBERT PATTERSON, Captain.
JOHN HENRY, Lieutenant.
JAMES PORTER, Ensign.
ALLEN CARTER, Sergeant.
GEORGE T. ASHBURN, Sergeant.
GRAVES GUNN, Sergeant.

FRANCIS PORTER, Sergeant.
GEORGE HICKMAN, Corporal.
ALLEN KUYKENDALL, Corporal.
WILLIAM BAILEY, Corporal.
ROBERT HENRY, Corporal.

Albert, Jacob,
Allen, Andrew,
Barrett, Enoch D.,
Brian, William,
Barringer, Jonathan,
Barnett, James,
Brown, Richard,
Burchfield, Thomas,
Brown, William,
Brown, Jimmy,
Bailey, James,
Clawson, John,
Collins, Dixon,
Coleman, Archibald,
Clevenger, Asa,
Caradine, David,
Cooksey, Warren,
Collins, Hollen,
Carlisle, Mathew,
Diamond, John,
Diamond, James,
Elam, John,
Finley, Andrew,

Ford, John,
Farmer, Gray B.,
Glister, Thomas,
Gist, William,
Gidcomb, John,
Gibson, Jordan,
Gilky, Thomas,
Henderson, Carnes D.,
Haney, Joseph,
Hodge, Nathan,
Hadden, William,
Hunsucker, Samuel,
Holley, William,
Jameson, Andrew,
Kown, Andrew,
Kenedy, Neil,
Kuykendall, Mark,
Larkins, Joseph,
Land, Lewis,
Land, Moses,
Morris, William,
McFarland, William D.,
Moore, Jeremiah,

Mann, John,
Miller, John,
Mitchell, Blake,
Neebart, Alexander,
Page, William,
Porter, Oliver,
Ralls, Robert,
Ralls, Green,
Smith, Ezekiel,
Sears, Abraham,
Smith, Joseph,
Smith, Asa,
Steele, Moses,
Thomas, John,
Thomas, Thomas,
Taylor, Peter,
Tannehill, Benjamin,
Williams, David,
Wheeler, Seburn,
Woods, William,
Wilson, Benjamin,
Wood, Peter.

194

II

ROLL OF FIELD AND STAFF, SLAUGHTER'S REGIMENT, KENTUCKY DETACHED MILITIA, WAR OF 1812, COMMANDED BY LIEUTENANT-COLONEL GABRIEL SLAUGHTER

GABRIEL SLAUGHTER, Lieutenant-colonel.
LANTY ARMSTRONG, First Major.
WILLIAM WAKEFIELD, Second Major.
SAMUEL MACOUN, Lieutenant.
WILLIAM RODES, Lieutenant.
ROGER THOMPSON, Lieutenant.
HORATIO GAITHER, Surgeon.
ROBERT H. C. PEARSON, S. Mate.

GEORGE C. BERRY, S. Mate.
THOMAS CURRY, Sergeant-major.
STROTHER H. GAINES, Quartermaster-sergeant.
JOHN THOMPSON, Assistant Quarterm'r.
THOMAS WITHER, Fife Major.
ABNER DECKER, Drum Major.

CAPTAIN GEORGE McAFEE'S COMPANY

GEORGE McAFEE, Captain.
WILLIAM BOHAN, Lieutenant.
JOHN M. JORDAN, Ensign.
JOHN LEWIS, Orderly Sergeant.
JULIUS RUCKER, Sergeant.
JAMES PIERSON, Sergeant.

SAMUEL R. TROUER, Sergeant.
JOHN COCHRAN, Sergeant.
ANDERSON POWERS, Corporal.
DANIEL BOHAN, Corporal.
DANIEL HAY, Corporal.
THOMAS ROBARDS, Corporal.

PRIVATES

Adams, Alexander,
Barnes, Zachariah,
Brim, Landy,
Brown, Thomas,
Bunton, Samuel,
Bradshaw, James L.,
Berns, Philip,
Bryant, Daniel,
Bradley, Jacob,
Barclay, David,
Cummings, Alexander,
Curry, Thomas,
Combs, Joseph,
Cummings, Abraham,
Coovert, Simon,
Curry, James,

Cooney, James,
Cooney, Daniel,
Davis, George,
Dean, William,
Dodson, George,
Dunklin, William,
Ellis, Daniel,
Foreman, Jacob,
Goodnight, Alexander,
Green, William,
Gilmore, Joseph,
Gabbert, James,
Harlow, Thomas,
Haley, Edmund,
Hulton, John,
Horn, John,

Horn, Philip,
Hall, Barnet,
Johnston, William,
Jones, William,
Jones, Thornton,
Kirkham, Joseph,
Knox, George C.,
Kirkpatrick, James,
Lytle, Lewis,
Lockhart, Levi,
Lewis, Elijah,
Lister, Cornelius,
Lister, Stephen,
McAfee, Samuel,
McDonald, Clement,
McCoy, Joseph,

McMinny, William,
Mullikin, John,
Montfort, Jacob,
Mitchel, Jacob,
Napier, William,
Poulter, Joseph,
Pierson, Joseph,
Philips, Aaron,
Preston, George,
Quigley, John,
Ray, William,
Rynierson, Jacob,
Rains, Allen,
Roberts, William,

Ruby, Jacob,
Robertson, Samuel,
Roberts, James,
Silyers, John,
Short, James,
Short, William,
Shields, William,
Sams, Russell,
Sample, James,
Short, Coleman,
Sally, Rany S.,
Stone, Levi,
Thomas, Thompson,
Towner, Samuel,

Thompson, George P.,
Toomy, Isaac,
Thomas, Edmund G.,
Voris, John,
Violet, Sinclair,
Walker, John,
Wilson, John H.,
Wells, John, sr.,
Wilson, Anthony,
Wells, John, jr.,
Whitberry, Jacob,
Weathers, Thomas,
Yest, Jacob.

CAPTAIN JOHN EVANS' COMPANY

JOHN EVANS, Captain.
JOHN CUPPINHEIFER, Lieutenant.
ROBERT GILMORE, Ensign.
AARON BARROW, Sergeant.
THOMAS GALLIWAY, Sergeant.
JOSEPH HEDRICK, Sergeant.

GEORGE DUNCAN, Sergeant.
JOHN EVANS, Corporal.
JOHN BURKE, Corporal.
WILLIAM McCULLOUGH, Corporal.
THOMAS NICHOLS, Corporal.

PRIVATES

Barker, Thomas,
Bebber, John,
Beadle, Seaton,
Barnet, James,
Barnet, Jubille,
Bowmer, William,
Burns, Mathew,
Burman, James,
Bowen, William,
Briant, Morgan,
Collins, Andrew,
Dishmon, James,
Dick, Archibald,
Dove, James,
Evans, John,
Elkins, Richard,
Floyd, Thomas,

Fitzpatrick, Samuel,
Fitzpatrick, George,
Gough, John,
Gilmore, William,
Griffin, John,
Gregory, Samuel,
Hargus, Thomas,
Herrin, Joel,
Hendrickson, Thomas,
Hendrickson, Gibson,
Hardister, William,
Hargus, John,
Harp, Westley,
Harmons, Jesse,
Hedrick, Jacob, jr.,
Hudson, Robert,
Hudson, Manoah,

Hedrick, Jacob, sr.,
Hanes, Ezekiah,
Hunt, William,
Hamilton, James,
Humphries, David,
Hunt, Samuel,
Johnson, James,
James, Daniel F.,
Jasper, Andrew,
McAllister, John,
Moody, Martin,
McCarty, William,
McCan, William,
McKaughan, William,
Neal, Isaac,
Preston, William,
Price, John,

Reagan, William,
Ridge, Robertson,
Riley, William,
Sneed, John,
Stroud, Ansel,
Tartar, Frederick,

White, Edward,
White, Elisha,
Woolsey, Thomas,
White, David,
Weatherman, Simon,

Wilson, Bird,
Weddle, George,
Weddle, John,
Wright, Walter,
White, John.

CAPTAIN LEONARD P. HIGDON'S COMPANY

LEONARD P. HIGDON, Captain.
DAVID HUSTON, Lieutenant.
JOHN YOUNG, Ensign.
SAMUEL HANDLEY, Orderly Sergeant.
WILLIAM BAILEY, First Sergeant.
BARTON HAWLEY, Second Sergeant.

FRANCIS HAGAN, Third Sergeant.
JAMES W. TYLER, Fourth Sergeant.
ISAAC ANDERSON, Corporal.
JAMES McDANIEL, Corporal.
HENRY HOLTZCLAW, Corporal.
NATHANIEL HARRIS, Corporal.

PRIVATES

Audd, Ambrose,
Anderson, Samuel,
Bredwell, Noah,
Bowl, James,
Burkhead, Isaac,
Blanford, Francis,
Baldwin, McKinsey,
Bishop, Solomon,
Brown, Frederick,
Blann, James,
Burkhead, Basil,
Basey, Jesse,
Bevin, Walter,
Bean, Judson,
Baldwin, Samuel,
Brown, James,
Connor, James,
Clark, Zacheus,
Cissel, James,
Coffman, Michael,
Calvert, Thomas,
Cane, Michael,
Clark, John,
Clemens, Thomas,
Connell, Hiram,

Connolly, Basil,
Cosby, Overton,
Clark, Abner,
DeMorgan, Reuben N.,
Drake, Jacob,
Dunn, Simpson,
Davis, Lemuel,
David, Amos,
Elliot, Greenbury,
Foxworthy, George,
Fox, William,
Fowler, Thomas,
Gibson, Henry,
Hanon, Ezekiel,
Harrison, Grove,
Hansford, William,
Hagerman, Tunis,
Higdon, James,
Hibbs, John,
Hall, Philip,
Knott, Henry,
Lefler, John,
Lent, William,
Lane, Benjamin,
McDaniel, Redman,

McLaughlin, Jesse,
Malon, Jacob,
McDaniel, William,
Miles, Francis,
Magnill, Richard,
McDaniel, John,
Osborn, Samuel,
Parrish, Francis,
Popham, Hawkins,
Popham, William,
Paul, James,
Polk, James,
Rynearson, Peter,
Roberts, George,
Rozner, William,
Smither, Joel,
Smith, John,
Turner, Joseph,
Vinson, George,
Witherton, John,
Wise, John,
Wise, Joseph,
Watson, Joseph,
Wilson, Benjamin

CAPTAIN JONATHAN OWSLEY'S COMPANY

Jonathan Owsley, Captain.
Loftis Cook, Lieutenant.
Stephen Lyons, Ensign.
Samuel P. Magill, Sergeant.
Henry Sharp, Sergeant.
John Logan, Sergeant.

John Gilbreath, Sergeant.
John Wood, Sergeant.
William Forsythe, Corporal.
Robert Bryant, Corporal.
John Huff, Corporal.
Thomas Scott, Corporal.

PRIVATES

Adams, Edward,
Bettis, John,
Bower, Francis,
Bryant, William,
Burnett, Nicholas,
Berry, Labon S.,
Ball, Isaiah,
Brook, John,
Baldwin, Joseph.
Burton, William,
Bowman, Jacob,
Breden, James,
Coombs, John,
Cox, Leroy,
Cavenaugh, Philemon,
Cash, William,
Dudarar, Coonrod,
Dudar, William,
Dodson, Thomas,
Davis, Nathan,
Doolin, James,
Davis, John,
Dasswell, Jesse,
Duncan, William,
Embree, Elijah,
Etone, Elijah.

Ervin, Francis,
Edwards, Peter,
Forsythe, David,
Goodnight, John,
Gooch, Roland,
Gibson, John,
Gill, Angel,
Hill, Zachariah,
Hotzclaw, Benjamin,
Hackley, James,
Hair, John,
Hutson, Lodrick,
Harvey, James W.,
Haynes, James,
Holmes, George,
Hall, James,
Jackson, William,
Low, Thomas,
Lavinder, John,
Lawrence, Hugh,
Lynn, James,
Martin, William,
McRoberts, Andrew,
McMullen, John,
McCrutcheon, William,

McManny, Charles,
Newcomb, Wilson,
Nelly, Edward,
Oalder, Jonathan,
Pettit, Walker,
Pence, John,
Parsons, Obediah,
Prewitt, David,
Ray, Joseph,
Renalds, Fountain,
Roberts, James,
Ross, Thomas J.,
Raybourne, John,
Simpson, John,
Sutton, Walker,
Souder, Jefferson,
Spratt, Thomas,
Singleton, McIntire,
Stephens, John,
Singleton, Thomas,
Tedrick, Jacob,
Warden, William,
Wade, Jeremiah,
Wood, William,
Warren, Burris.

CAPTAIN JOHN FARMER'S COMPANY

John Farmer, Captain.
Willoughby Ashby, Lieutenant.
John Figg, Ensign.
Jesse Keeth, First Sergeant.
David Weller, First Sergeant.
Isaac Chambers, First Sergeant.

Isaac Houston, Second Sergeant.
Owen R. Griffith, Third Sergeant.
Corcelius Woods, Fourth Sergeant.
Samuel Heffler, First Corporal.
Barnard Bridwell, Second Corporal.
George Weller, Third Corporal.

198

Angel, George,
Anderson, Thomas,
Anderson, John,
Berton, William,
Bright, John,
Brown, Robert,
Bennett, Jery,
Brewer, James,
Boly, Peter,
Carter, William,
Carico, James,
Chaplain, Jery,
Carter, Samuel,
Carter, Joseph,
Conor, George,
Cane, Mathew,
Doneheu, James,
Denbow, James,
Davis, Jesse,
Dewitt, Abraham,
Davis, John,

Gilkey, William,
Grubb, William,
Glass, James H.,
Hampton, David,
Hill, Robert,
Harder, John,
Huffman, George,
Hagan, Dory,
Ice, James,
Jones, Joseph,
Jones, John,
Johnston, William,
Johnston, Joseph,
Kenny, William,
Keth, Isaac,
Low, Richard,
Lerit, Joseph,
Lanam, James,
Mattingly, Edward,
Medcalf, James,

Medcalf, Benjamin,
Marshall, Daniel,
Miller, Frederick,
Micater, Patrick,
Philips, George,
Powers, Richard,
Reed, Richard,
Robinson, Alexander,
Spilman, Henry,
Springston, Abraham,
Sinkhorn, William,
Shaream, George,
Seals, John,
Thompson, James,
Thompson, John,
Walker, Howard,
White, John,
White, Francis,
Wilcox, Isaac,
York, John.

CAPTAIN ADAM VICKERY'S COMPANY

ADAM VICKERY, Captain.
JOHN GARNER, Lieutenant.
JOHN BARROW, Ensign.
HIRAM GREGORY, Sergeant.
THOMAS BROWN, Sergeant.
MOSES BARNES, Sergeant.

ALEXANDER BROWN, Sergeant.
HARMAN ELROD, Sergeant.
WILLIAM HURT, Corporal.
GEORGE DODSON, Corporal.
THOMAS RYON, Corporal.
LAPSLY HALL, Corporal.

Ard, James,
Andrew, Alexander,
Acre, Peter,
Burnham, Owen,
Bell, John,
Ballard, John,
Burnet, James,
Baker, James,
Baker, Stephen,
Barnes, William,
Bowman, Willis,

Barnes, Enos,
Brown, Lewis,
Brown, Barnabus,
Butrim, Cornelius,
Craig, John H.,
Casson, John,
Caughorn, William,
Cook, Enos,
Cox, David,
Cooper, Caleb,
Duffey, John,

Dean, James,
Davis, William,
Dabney, Charles,
Elrod, Adam,
Foster, John,
Gray, Jesse,
Gholson, Samuel,
Gibson, Stephen,
Gooding, Abraham,
Gibson, Thomas,
Hains, John,

199

Hill, William,
Hall, Henry,
Hill, Claiborn,
Keniday, John,
Kogan, William,
Lea, John,
Luster, John,
Lenn, James,
Lambert, Henry,
Livingston, Robert,
Miller, George,
McGown, Solomon,
Mills, Ulissius,
Moore, David,

Mays, David,
Neal, Jesse,
Pow, Alexander,
Ray, John,
Southword, John,
Shaw, John,
Shelton, John,
Savage, John,
Shelton, James,
Smith, William,
Stephens, Peter,
Smith, Henry,
Stephens, Thomas,
Smith, George,

Sallee, William I.,
Tiller, John,
Thornton, John,
Thomas, Samuel,
Wade, John,
Willice, John,
Woods, James,
Welsher, Joshua,
West, Joseph,
Welsher, Josiah,
West, Alexander,
Wade, Elisha,
Wray, Daniel,
Wallace, Barnabus.

CAPTAIN WILLIAM WOOD'S COMPANY

WILLIAM WOOD, Captain.
PETER OATMAN, Lieutenant.
THOMAS BROWN, Ensign.
HENRY ROBINSON, Sergeant.
ABSALOM RICE, Sergeant.
GEORGE HERRING, Sergeant.

ISAAC THERMAN, Sergeant.
THOMAS JONES, Sergeant.
JOHN McKINSEY, Corporal.
JOHN ALLEN, Corporal.
SIMON MOBELY, Corporal.
JOHN BOURNE, Corporal.

PRIVATES

Anderson, Garland,
Anderson, Thomas,
Adams, John,
Blankenship, John,
Brown, Stanton,
Bailey, Lewis,
Beech, Joel,
Brown, William,
Burton, Allen,
Brown, Edwin,
Barron, Mathias,
Barker, Richard,
Boadly, Peter D.,
Brown, John,
Clements, Thomas,
Coy, Samuel,
Chambers, Abraham,
Coy, Thomas,
Clark, William,

Davidson, John,
Duggins, Richard,
Dooly, Jacob,
Duncan, George,
Dotson, Thomas,
Edens, Mathew,
Elliott, Reuben,
Erton, Henry,
Graham, Robinson,
Gill, John,
Greenstaff, George,
Garvin, William,
Green, Thomas,
Gromer, Henry,
Gayheart, Isaac,
Hotsclaw, Martin,
Horley, William,
Hurd, William,
Hay, Isaac,

Huffman, Henry,
Henderson, Joseph,
Hicks, Fleming,
Hoskins, Samuel,
Holmes, Isaac,
Jackman, Thomas,
Lampton, William,
McMeas, Jacob,
Martendale, Moses,
McFadgin, James,
Moore, Moses,
Miller, James,
Mayfield, Sutherland,
Naylor, Jesse,
Newcomb, Lance,
Naylor, George T.,
Naylor, John,
Pow, William,
Pollard, Abner,

Preston, John,
Pucket, William,
Spencer, John,
Stone, James,
Stanton, Fleming,
Skiler, John,
Stephens, William,
Stephens, ———.

Thacker, Elijah,
Turpin, James,
Tarrett, Larkin,
Tunge:, Benjamin,
Vance Jacob,
Weather, John,
Warren, Joseph,

Wiley, Benjamin,
Woodal, John,
Warmouth, Thomas,
Warmouth, Githean,
Williams, Oscar,
Williams, George,
Yancy, George.

CAPTAIN WILLIAM WADE'S COMPANY

WILLIAM WADE, Captain.
JOHN RIFFE, Lieutenant.
MATHEW COFFEE, Ensign.
DAVID JOHNSON, Sergeant.
JOSHUA MOORE, Sergeant.
JOHN D. THURMOND, Sergeant.

JOHN SPEARS, Sergeant.
JOHN SHANNON, Sergeant.
WILLIAM JONES, Corporal.
JOHN ESTIS, Corporal.
STARLING COULTER, Corporal.
JACOB CUNNINGHAM, Corporal.

PRIVATES

(Obinion or) Albanion, Geo.
Barnett, Skuyler,
Carmen, William,
Curdum, William,
Coxe, Joseph,
Carter, Moses,
Cloyd, Joseph,
Charlton, Levi,
Coulter, Morris,
Carman, Ezekiah,
Clifton, Nehemiah,
Clifton, Isaiah,
Cinkhous, Henry,
Cunningham, Thomas,
Clark, Thomas,
Dyer, William,
Duncan, Flemmin,
Dobbs, William,
Drummond, James,
Davenport, Thomas,
East, Nimrod,
Ewebank, James,
Ecten, Charles,
Edwards, Aaron,
Ellis, John,

Figg, William,
Gentry, Benjamin,
Gee, John,
Hite, Burton,
Harvey, Robert,
Harvel, Squire,
Hutcherson, Samuel,
Johnson, Luke,
King, Thomas,
Linthicum, Thomas,
Lee, Francis,
Lee, Joseph P.,
McCutchan, Samuel,
Minor, Laban,
Mason, James,
McWherton, Jesse,
Mason, Thomas,
McCan, William,
Mason, Thomson,
Northcut, Arthur,
Noble, Thomas,
Pankey John B.,
Price, Robert,
Royaltree, Henry,
Riffe, Christopher,

Ragsdale, Gabriel,
Royaltree, William,
Riffe, Abraham,
Reed, Philip,
Routsaw, Coonrod,
Raglin, James,
Reed, Little B.,
Studer, David,
Seabron, Jehu,
Stepp, William,
Selch, Nicholas,
Skidmore, John,
Snow, John,
Studor, Randal,
Stanton, William,
Thomas, Robert,
Tailor, Jacob,
Vorus, Abraham,
Vautres, Jacob,
Williams, Amos,
Wright, Bennett C.,
Whitesides, David,
Williams, Richard,
Yager, Lewis.

201

CAPTAIN EDWARD BERRY'S COMPANY

EDWARD BERRY, Captain.
DAVID RODMAN, Lieutenant.
THOMAS McINTIRE, Ensign.
STEPHEN THOMPSON, Sergeant.
GEORGE ELLIOTT, Sergeant.
STARLING THOMPSON, Sergeant.

CHARLES FOWLER, Sergeant.
JOHN AUSTIN, Sergeant.
ANDREW POWEL, Sergeant.
JOEL NELSON, Sergeant.
PHILIP RICHARDSON, Sergeant.
JOHN McCLURE, Sergeant.

PRIVATES

Adams, Henry,
Burns, Isaac,
Bennett, George W.,
Baker, James,
Baker, William,
Bryan, John,
Barnett, William,
Champion, Joseph,
Cannon, Robert,
Cogenom, George,
Campton, James,
Casey, David,
Catlin, Seth,
Carter, Benjamin,
Cross, William,
Creagh, Christian,
Davis, Robert,
Earl, Samuel,
Ferguson, Daniel,
Franklin, Edward,
Graves, John,
Hickerson, John,
Hickerson, Joseph,
Hilton, Henry,
Hart, William,

Higgins, David,
Jackson, James,
Lockett, Samuel,
Lannom, Lewis,
Lawson, Chester,
Lawson, Berry,
Lambert, David,
Lannom, Samuel,
Miles, Alexander,
Miller, Joseph,
Morgan, Abraham,
McMurry, Thomas,
Maxwell, Charles,
Morris, Reuben,
Matherly, Joel,
Malone, William,
Milbourn, Israel,
McMurry, William,
Mann, William,
McAllister, James,
Mead, Joseph,
McMurry, William,
McAllister, Daniel,
Miles, Edward,
Montgomery, Thomas,

Nelson, William,
Oldridge, Nathaniel,
Prewitt, Daniel,
Prater, Reson,
Richards, Zodick,
Ridge, Cornelius,
Ridge, William,
Right, Robert,
Right, William,
Reed, Nathan,
Seamster, Pleasant,
Simpson, Floyd,
Stump, Johnston,
Simpson, Asa,
Taylor, Jeremiah,
Tolby, Jonathan,
Whitter, William,
Watham, James H.,
White, Thomas L.,
Watham, Nicholas,
Whitten, Jeremiah,
Whitehouse, John,
Whitehouse, Cornelius,
Woods, Henry.

CAPTAIN WILLIAM PHILIPS' COMPANY

WILLIAM PHILIPS, Captain.
GODHART SMACK, Lieutenant.
JOHN LUDWICK, Ensign.
ASA R. HILL, Sergeant.
JOSEPH ABEL, Sergeant.
WILLIAM McENERY, Sergeant.
CHARLES COLTER, Sergeant.

HENRY COWAN, Sergeant.
ROBERT ROCHESTER, Corporal.
JOHN GRAYHAM, Corporal.
JOHN MOBLEY, Corporal.
ROBERT BRUMFIELD, Corporal.
THOMAS HILL, Musician.
WILLIAM VANOY, Musician.

Anderson, Thomas,
Blaire, James,
Brown, Francis,
Brown, Henderson,
Bullott, John,
Butler, William,
Botains, William, sr.,
Botains, William, jr.,
Baker, Henry,
Blacketler, William,
Camburn, Osburn,
Cissell, Thomas,
Cidwell, John,
Caho, John,
Cissell, Robert,
Cannon, Israel,
Cravens, James,
Cunstable, Stephen,
Cinkborn, John,
Cundiff, James,
Cartico, Lloyd,
Collier, Daniel,
Easton, John,
Elliott, John,
Enson, George,

Green, Charles,
Gerton, John,
Grey, Charles,
Galesby, Edward,
Gains, Strother H.,
Harris, Overton,
Harris, William,
Hinton, Shadrick,
Howard, Charles,
Hall, Thomas,
Knott, Jeremiah,
Landers, James,
Lyons, John,
Lyons, Charles W.,
Lanham, William,
Lockman, John B.,
Lockman, Charles,
Mercer, Martin,
Mills, Samuel,
Mattingly, Joseph,
Mahoney, William,
Miller, Ignatius,
Marby, Micajah,
Morgan, Jubel,

Meanally, Basil,
Meanally, John,
Mitchel, Jacob,
Newton, Ignatius,
Nichols, John,
Owings, James,
Patterson, Joseph,
Philips, Jesse,
Quigans, James,
Quigans, Joseph,
Stemmons, Henry,
Stanfield, John,
Smithers, Daniel,
Smith, Richard,
Simpson, Allugus,
Smith, John,
Sanders, John,
Updergrove, Joseph,
Vessels, Benjamin,
Vaun, Obediah,
Waid, Evan,
Wooley, John,
Williams, Edward,
Whitehouse, Thomas.

ROLL OF FIELD AND STAFF, DAVIS'S REGIMENT, KENTUCKY DETACHED MILITIA, WAR OF 1812, COMMANDED BY LIEUTENANT-COLONEL PRESLEY GRAY

PRESLEY GRAY, Lieutenant-colonel.
JOHN DAVIS, Major.
JAMES JOHNSON, Major.
WILLIAM WALKER, Major.
ZEBA HOLT, Major.
S. C. STEPHENS, Adjutant.
GEORGE P. MILLER, Paymaster.
ZACHARIAH TERRYHEL, Quartermaster.
ALLEN A. HAMILTON, Surgeon.

HENRY WINSLOW, Surgeon's Mate.
WILLIAM W. FORD, Sergeant-major.
SAMUEL STEWART, S. Mate.
WILLIAM VANCLEVE, Drum Major.
JOHN CURRY, Fife Major.
SAMUEL GRAY, Quartermaster-sergeant.
SAMUEL BLACKWELL, Quartermaster-sergeant.

CAPTAIN ROBERT THRUSTON'S COMPANY

ROBERT THRUSTON, Captain.
HENRY GRESHAM, Lieutenant.
JOHN D. GOTT, Ensign.
SAMUEL S. GREEN, Sergeant.
DANIEL RAGSDALE, Sergeant.
JOHN S. SIMPSON, Sergeant.
AARON COLLETT, Sergeant.

GEORGE RUNGER, Corporal.
ADAM GILLILAND, Corporal.
ISAAC HILL, Corporal.
DAVID RICHEY, Corporal.
JOHN CURRY, Fifer.
THOMAS CURRY, Drummer.

PRIVATES

Armstrong, Benjamin,
Arnold, William,
Arnold, Robert,
Allen, Nathaniel,
Alexander, John,
Blanton, Thomas,
Bowman, James,
Bryant, Thomas,
Brooky, John,
Barnett, Philip E.,
Blanchard, John,
Caldwell, William,

Cathran, John,
Cooley, Jesse,
Clark, David,
Crow, Andrew,
Chenowith, Thomas,
Collett, Moses,
Caplinger, John,
Cottonham, John D.,
Daniels, George,
Dawville, Charles,
Elsbury, Jonathan,
Farmer, James,

Galbreath, William,
Hunter, Charles,
Hunter, Willis,
Hill, John,
Ingraham, James,
Inshmeyer, John,
Knapp, Charles,
Kirk, James,
Kincade, Matthew,
Lowell, Jacob,
Leggett, John,
Miller, Christopher,

Messen, James,
Milam, John,
McCartney, Andrew,
Newell, Archibald,
Osborn, John,
Porter, James,
Pittenger, Thomas,
Prewett, Joel,
Parsons, David,
Penley, Wesley,

Russell, John,
Ragsdale, Frederick,
Robinson, James,
Shrum, John,
Sharp, William,
Standiford, William,
Smith, Henry,
Spence, Willis,
Stillwell, Isaiah,

Stafford, Thomas,
Tyler, Willis,
Taylor, James,
Tadlock, Alexander,
Thursby, James,
Weems, James S.,
White, Warren,
Woodward, John,
Washburn, Samuel S.

CAPTAIN THOMAS JOYES' COMPANY

THOMAS JOYES, Captain.
ANDREW PORTTORFF, Lieutenant.
SAMUEL EARICKSON, Ensign.
JOHN HADLEY, Sergeant.
WILLIAM SALE, Sergeant.
JOHN BOOKER, Sergeant.

JOHN W. BAINBRIDGE, Sergeant.
JOHN RAY, Corporal.
JOHN O. HANLON, Corporal.
WILLIAM DUERSON, Corporal.
ABNER C. YOUNG, Corporal.

PRIVATES

Ames, Robert B.,
Brinley, Jacob,
Bateman, Isaac,
Balee, Abraham,
Booty, John,
Brandenburgh, Absalom,
Bagwell, John,
Croxton, Cornelius,
Carson, Hugh,
Cardwell, William,
Carlton, Francis D.,
Crossgrave, Charles,
Calhoun, Alexander,
Dunn, Thomas,
Davis, Squire,
Dougherty, Patrick,
Elms, William,
Floyd, Nathaniel,
Gosshort, Adam,
Greenawalt, John,
Glassgow, James,
Glassgow, John,

Guthrie, Moses,
Hilliard, Anson G.,
Hill, Mason,
Hubbs, Jacob,
Holt, Samuel,
Johnson, William,
Jones, John,
Jackson, George,
Kelly, Christopher,
Lashbrook, Samuel,
Martin, Westley,
Meddis, Godfrey,
Morlow, Peter,
Miller, John,
Merryfield, John,
Miller, Levi,
Myrtle, William,
Miller, George,
Mayfield, Isaac,
Morrow, John,
Minter, John,

Meddis, John, (Waiter)
Newkirk, William,
Ormer, Peter,
Parish, Price,
Pearson, George R.,
Pierce, Chester,
Ralston, Alexander,
Risley, James,
Ross, Thomas,
Stewart, James,
Stower, Patrick,
Slaughter, Jacob,
Stout, Michael,
Talbot, Thomas,
Thickston, William,
Tyler, Joseph,
Traceler, Philip,
Williams, Moses,
Woodward, James,
Wheeler, Jesse,
Welsh, Moses.

205

CAPTAIN WILLIAM WALKER'S COMPANY

WILLIAM WALKER, Captain.
JOHN SMITH, Lieutenant.
JOHN WEBB, Ensign.
JOHN HARVEY, Sergeant.

JOHN H. GIBBS, Sergeant.
JOEL HARDIN, Sergeant.
ELIJAH YORK, Sergeant.

PRIVATES

Arterbury, James,
Bear, John,
Benedict, Tomkins,
Bear, Adam,
Bear, George,
Burgman, William,
Bates, Simeon,
Brewer, Charles,
Brown, Asa,
Carr, Elijah,
Clarke, Albin,
Cashman, Peter,
Cashman, John,
Case, Jacob,
Cowper, Joshua,
Caffrey, Thomas M.,
Clayton, John,
Davis, Silas,
Dawson, John,
Dowddle, Thomas J.,
Gardner, James,

Gilblaine, Robert,
Goatly, Thomas,
Gentry, William,
Glasscock, William,
Horton, Anthony,
Hulse, Josiah,
Holmes, Nicholas,
Hedges, Robert,
Hayes, Daniel,
Jarboe, Joseph,
Jackson, Isaac,
Johns, John,
Kindor, Peter,
King, John,
Keith, Jacob,
Langsley, John,
Liney, Zachariah,
Lyons, John,
Mattingly, Bennett,
Morgan, Lambeth,

Mellor, Jacob,
Millor, John,
Night, John,
Osten, Jeremiah,
Parpoint, Charles,
Pate, Allen,
Painter, William,
Pile, Francis,
Paul, George,
Pearman, Samuel,
Pearman, John,
Pate, Jeremiah,
Padden, John,
Radley, Ichabod,
Sally, Oliver P.,
Sevaney, Glasberry,
Slack, William,
Thomas, Joseph,
White, William,
Whitaker, Jesse.

CAPTAIN JOSEPH FUNK'S COMPANY

JOSEPH FUNK, Captain.
THOMAS TODD, Lieutenant.
MARTIN ADAMS, Ensign.
WILLIAM WALLACE, Sergeant.
ISAAC CARR, Sergeant.
JAMES AUSTIN, Sergeant.

JOSEPH WILLHORT, Sergeant.
FREDERICK MASON, Corporal.
JAMES PREWITT, Corporal.
JOHN YOUNG, Corporal.
THOMAS BATEMAN, Corporal.
WILLIAM TETER, Corporal.

PRIVATES

Anderson, Thomas,
Archer, Thomas,
Austin, William,
Austin, Daniel,
Bateman, John,

Briser, James,
Blankinboke, Jacob,
Brooks, Jacob,
Cann, Edward,
Campbell, James,

Campbell, George B.,
Crews, Elijah,
Crews, Zachariah,
Crow, Andrew D.,
Cox, George,

206

Edmondson, John,
Fiteshue, Cole,
Fitzer, Jacob,
Ferguson, Samuel,
Forus, James,
Gilman, Timothy,
Griffy, Samuel,
Greathouse, Luther,
Green, Joseph,
Gunn, Jonathan,
Green, John,
Harris, Thomas,
Hendricks, James F.,
Hortly, John,
Hensely, Alexander,
Harmond, John,
Hobson, Milburn.

Ingram, James,
Jones, Hamilton,
Job, Andrew,
Jones, Thomas,
Johnson, Thomas,
Kalfers, Jacob,
Knight, John,
Louther, Henry,
Leggett, William,
Maxwell, William,
Mitchell, William,
Miller, Adam,
Pearce, John,
Powell, William,
Portlow, Samuel,
Portlow, Edward,
Rudy, George.

Shelman, Jacob,
Spalding, George W.,
Steel, Andrew,
Stuart, Robert,
Shake, John,
Shake, Adam,
Shirley, Absalom,
Tyler, David,
Tyler, Absalom,
Williams, Benjamin,
Willhoit, Larkin,
Wilky, John,
Wood, Timothy,
Wood, Henry,
Wooden, Robert,
Woodward, Michael.

CAPTAIN ZIBA HOLT'S COMPANY

ZIBA HOLT, Captain.
JOHN MONTGOMERY, Lieutenant.
ADAM MOWNY, Ensign.
WYAT COLEMAN, Sergeant.
WILLIAM STEWART, Sergeant.
HENRY BLUNT, Sergeant.

JOHN HOLODY, Sergeant.
THOMAS SUBLETT, Corporal.
JOSEPH PEW, Corporal.
NATHAN CHALFRANT, Corporal.
MARK WILLIAMS, Corporal.
JEREMIAH STOWERS, Fifer.

PRIVATES

Anderson, Josiah,
Agins, John,
Baker, Joseph,
Brasher, Reason,
Boon, Moses,
Brown, William,
Bags, John,
Barnhill, William,
Brent, James,
Barker, Samuel,
Colvin, James M.,
Chase, William,
Conway, William,
Corin, William,
Crews, Jeremiah,
Dermit, James,

Drinkel, Timothy,
Dean, John,
Eallon, Charles,
Gillum Charles,
Glenn, John,
Gillum, Benjamin,
Gilpin, George,
Glass, John,
Holt, John,
Hammen, John,
Heath, Martin,
Horton, James,
Gentry, Pleasant,
Gibson, Perrygon,
Gannon, Zachariah,
Jones, Hamilton,

James, Thomas,
Jones, Moses,
Kindor, Peter,
Kendall, Thomas,
Keyton, John,
Lattey, Mathew,
Lock, Samuel,
McGee, William,
Miller, William,
Montgomery, Robert,
McGannon, Thomas,
Overton, Moses,
Parrott, William,
Parker, Asa,
Reastine, John,
Reed, James,

Ragsdale, William,
Robbins, David,
Redding, Samuel,
Senor, David,
Spencer, Ambrose,
Sparks, Walter,

Spillman, Charles,
Sparks, Henry,
Taylor, John,
Thomas, John,
Veal, Thomas,
Watson, Samuel,

Williams, John,
Waters, Major,
Williams, Samuel,
Wiley, Matthew,
Wooders, Stephen.

CAPTAIN WILLIAM GANAWAY'S COMPANY

WILLIAM GANAWAY, Captain.
JULIUS C. JACKSON, Lieutenant.
JOHN FIELD, Ensign.
JOHN CLEVER, Sergeant.
PETER BODINE, Sergeant.
SAMUEL C. MYERS, Sergeant.

HENRY LEACH, Sergeant.
SAMUEL KELLY, Corporal.
JOHN TRAVIS, Corporal.
JOHN COHEN, Corporal.
BENJAMIN THOMAS, Corporal.

PRIVATES

Anderson, Athel,
Bott, John,
Barron, Josiah,
Burnett, Abraham,
Barron, Thomas,
Barron, Shadrick,
Barnett, Felia,
Bennett, Briant,
Bartell, George,
Bennett, Reuben,
Brown, Isaac,
Brown, Henry,
Cane, John,
Conrad, Henry,
Collard, William,
Colaway, Walter,
Conrad, John,
Davis, George,

Dunlap, Henry,
Duff, William M.,
Evans, William,
Fulkerson, Adam,
Fulkerson, John,
Haycraft, James,
Hogan, George,
Harris, Samuel,
Islor, Jacob,
Jones, Lemuel,
Jones, Philip,
Jordan, James,
Kelly, George W.,
Kelly, Benjamin,
Lewellon, Jabez,
Lock, William,
Logsdon, James,
Moloham, Clement,

Myers, Benjamin,
Miller, Uriah,
Ogden, Zachariah,
Ogden, Levi,
Olvy, Thomas,
Olvy, Clement,
Ogden, James,
Philips, John,
Prunty, Robert,
Rice, Allen,
Spray, Jonas,
Sconse, John,
Tanner, Frederick,
Wakeland, William R.,
Ward, Jesse,
Williams, Evan,
Welcher, William,
Wood, Robert.

CAPTAIN JACOB PEACOCK'S COMPANY

JACOB PEACOCK, Captain.
BENJAMIN HENSON, Lieutenant.
JOHN KELLY, Ensign.
JOSEPH SWEARING, Sergeant.
JESSE BURCH, Sergeant.
BENJAMIN COLLINS, Sergeant.

JOHN SHIRKILIFFE, Sergeant.
WILLIAM TODD, Corporal.
LEVI RIDGWAY, Corporal.
JOSEPH RUDD, Corporal.
WALTER SMITH, Corporal.
CHARLES WILSON, Corporal.

Burdett, William,
Burdett, Benjamin,
Beam, George,
Baldwin, McKensey,
Blanford, George,
Bishop, Henry,
Craw, Joseph,
Campbell, Jacob,
Cummins, John,
Clark, Joseph,
Collins, Elisha,
Cardwell, George,
Charles, William,
Cosby, Ignatius,
Davis, John,
Dumont, Peter,
Danielson, William,
Duberry, Benjamin,
Duberry, James,
Easton, Samuel,

Glass, Royal,
Greenwell, John B.,
Harris, Essex,
Hardy, Jacob,
Hopewell, Thomas,
Herrin, James,
Johnson, Joseph,
Kerns, Daniel,
Kirk, William,
Kirke, Selerin,
Lashbrook, Thomas,
Merryman, Charles,
McArthur, John,
McDonald, Archibald,
Miller, Peter,
McDonnel, Miles,
McGary, Barney,
Martin, John,
Owens. George,

Osborn, Ezekiel,
Price, Samuel,
Polly, Joseph,
Pratt, Richard,
Pursley, Peter,
Quick, Ephraim,
Reed, Robert,
Rogers, John,
Rennels, Barney,
Shephard, William,
Shaw, William,
Steel, John,
Sligar, John,
Smock, Jacob,
Thompson, William,
Tonque, John B.,
Whalen, Joseph,
Waters, Hezekiah B.,
Younger, Ebenezer.

CAPTAIN ZACHARIAH TERRELL'S COMPANY

ZACHARIAH TERRELL, Captain.
DAVID ADAMS, Lieutenant.
JAMES PERRY, Ensign.
JAMES VANCE, First Sergeant.
JOSHUA RUTLEDGE, Second Sergeant.
JOHN BUCHANNON, Third Sergeant.
ISAAC HURD, Fourth Sergeant.

JACOB COOPERIDER, Corporal.
PETER POLLY, Corporal.
GILBERT FLANKINS, Corporal.
THOMAS FRAZIER, Corporal.
ELIJAH SUMMERS, Corporal.
JESSE ISAACS, Musician.

Armstrong, Richard,
Applegate, Elisha,
Burnett, William,
Bourne, Benjamin,
Briscoe, Warner,
Baker, Solomon,
Biggs, Hillery,
Blackwell, Samuel,
Bishop, Michael,
Blackwell, Robert,
Connelly, Rice,

Carico, Thomas,
Criswell, Robert,
Cardwell, John,
Corlin, Benjamin,
Dillon, John,
Dalgarn, Allen,
Deringer, Martin,
Davis, Jacob,
Davis, William,
Drake, John,
Ewin, Squire,

Edrington, John,
Floyd, Elijah,
Ford, John,
Gray, William,
Gouch, Nicholas,
Hollis, John P.,
Hogan, Isaac C.,
Hackworth, Joseph,
Harris, Samuel,
Jones, Rodham,
Jacobs, John,

Kirkindal, Henry,
Kipheart, Philip,
Lemaston, Ewin,
McGee, William,
Mudd, Francis,
Miller, Nathaniel,
Miller, Owen,
Myers, David,
Nelson, William,
Nelson, John,
Newman, Thomas,

Newman, John,
Neaver, Daniel,
Neville, James,
Neaves, William,
Paine, Elzy,
Roe, Nicholas,
Rodgers, John,
Runy, James,
Stutt, Christian,
Stodghill, Thomas,
Steel, William,

Sherburne, Pascal,
Sanders, Johnson,
Spencer, Thomas,
Steel, James,
Steel, Rankin,
Scott, James,
Todd, Samuel,
Terrill, John,
Vaniel, Henry,
Welch, William.

CAPTAIN AARON HART'S COMPANY

AARON HART, Captain.
MOSES HART, Lieutenant.
NATHAN TUCKER, Ensign.
ARTHUR McGAUGHEY, First Sergeant.
GEORGE SISS, Second Sergeant.
JOHN COLLINS, Third Sergeant.

JOHN BURRISS, Fourth Sergeant,
WILLIAM HUDDLESTON, Corporal.
WILLIAM WATKINS, Corporal.
DANIEL GREENWAIT, Corporal.
JAMES LINVILLE, Corporal.
DAVID WADDLE, Corporal.

PRIVATES

Alexander, Thomas,
Alexander, David B.,
Arrington, Lewis,
Bennett, James,
Bliss, Francis,
Blain, James,
Clark, Eaden,
Clark, James,
Case, Joseph,
Cash, Jeremiah,
Cast, John,

Daugherty, Allen,
Gaddy, John,
Guardman, Jonathan,
Grigsby, John,
Graham, John,
Huston, William,
Hornbeck, Isaac,
Hudgins, John,
Johnston, Thomas,
Killam, Samuel,
Lender, Abraham,

McContis, William,
Miller, Philip,
Price, William,
Snyder, Fielding,
Sipes, Henry,
Stokes, Joel,
Shipler, George,
Thomas, Owen,
Utterback, Jacob,
Utterback, Thomas,
Watkins, Hankerson.

LEONAUR

ALSO FROM LEONAUR
AVAILABLE IN SOFTCOVER OR HARDCOVER WITH DUST JACKET

CAMP-FIRE AND COTTON-FIELD by *Thomas W. Knox*—A New York Herald Correspondent's View of the American Civil War.

SERGEANT STILLWELL by *Leander Stillwell*—The Experiences of a Union Army Soldier of the 61st Illinois Infantry During the American Civil War.

STONEWALL'S CANNONEER by *Edward A. Moore*—Experiences with the Rockbridge Artillery, Confederate Army of Northern Virginia, During the American Civil War.

CONFEDERATE BLOCKADE RUNNER by *John Wilkinson*—The Personal Recollections of an Officer of the Confederate Navy.

THE SIXTH CORPS by *George Stevens*—The Army of the Potomac, Union Army, During the American Civil War.

THE RAILROAD RAIDERS by *William Pittenger*—An Ohio Volunteers Recollections of the Andrews Raid to Disrupt the Confederate Railroad in Georgia During the American Civil War.

CITIZEN SOLDIER by *John Beatty*—An Account of the American Civil War by a Union Infantry Officer of Ohio Volunteers Who Became a Brigadier General.

COX: PERSONAL RECOLLECTIONS OF THE CIVIL WAR--VOLUME 1 by *Jacob Dolson Cox*—West Virginia, Kanawha Valley, Gauley Bridge, Cotton Mountain, South Mountain, Antietam, the Morgan Raid & the East Tennessee Campaign.

COX: PERSONAL RECOLLECTIONS OF THE CIVIL WAR--VOLUME 2 by *Jacob Dolson Cox*—Siege of Knoxville, East Tennessee, Atlanta Campaign, the Nashville Campaign & the North Carolina Campaign.

THE RELUCTANT REBEL by *William G. Stevenson*—A young Kentuckian's experiences in the Confederate Infantry & Cavalry during the American Civil War.

KERSHAW'S BRIGADE VOLUME 1 by *D. Augustus Dickert*—Manassas, Seven Pines, Sharpsburg (Antietam), Fredricksburg, Chancellorsville, Gettysburg, Chickamauga, Chattanooga, Fort Sanders & Bean Station.

KERSHAW'S BRIGADE VOLUME 2 by *D. Augustus Dickert*—At the wilderness, Cold Harbour, Petersburg, The Shenandoah Valley and Cedar Creek.

HISTORY OF THE CAVALRY OF THE ARMY OF THE POTOMAC by *Charles D. Rhodes*—Including Pope's Army of Virginia and the Cavalry Operations in West Virginia During the American Civil War.

LEONAUR

ALSO FROM LEONAUR
AVAILABLE IN SOFTCOVER OR HARDCOVER WITH DUST JACKET

LIGHT BOB *by Robert Blakeney*—The experiences of a young officer in H.M 28th & 36th regiments of the British Infantry during the Peninsular Campaign of the Napoleonic Wars 1804 - 1814.

NAPOLEON'S RUSSIAN CAMPAIGN by *Philippe Henri de Segur*—The Invasion, Battles and Retreat by an Aide-de-Camp on the Emperor's Staff

SWORDS OF HONOUR by *Henry Newbolt & Stanley L. Wood*—The Careers of Six Outstanding Officers from the Napoleonic Wars, the Wars for India and the American Civil War. Illustrated.

HUSSAR IN WINTER by *Alexander Gordon*—A British Cavalry Officer during the retreat to Corunna in the Peninsular campaign of the Napoleonic Wars.

THE LIFE OF THE REAL BRIGADIER GERARD VOLUME 1 THE YOUNG HUSSAR 1782 - 1807 *by Jean-Baptiste De Marbot*—A French Cavalryman Of the Napoleonic Wars at Marengo, Austerlitz, Jena, Eylau & Friedland.

THE LIFE OF THE REAL BRIGADIER GERARD VOLUME 2 IMPERIAL AIDE-DE-CAMP 1807 - 1811 *by Jean-Baptiste De Marbot*—A French Cavalryman of the Napoleonic Wars at Saragossa, Landshut, Eckmuhl, Ratisbon, Aspern-Essling, Wagram, Busaco & Torres Vedras.

THE LIFE OF THE REAL BRIGADIER GERARD VOLUME 3 COLONEL OF CHASSEURS 1811 - 1815 by *Jean-Baptiste De Marbot*—A French Cavalryman in the retreat from Moscow, Lutzen, Bautzen, Katzbach, Leipzig, Hanau & Waterloo.

RIFLEMAN COSTELLO by *Edward Costello*—The adventures of a soldier of the 95th (Rifles) in the Peninsular & Waterloo Campaigns of the Napoleonic wars.

WITH THE LIGHT DIVISION by *John H. Cooke*—The Experiences of an Officer of the 43rd Light Infantry in the Peninsula and South of France During the Napoleonic Wars.

COLBORNE: A SINGULAR TALENT FOR WAR by *John Colborne*—The Napoleonic Wars Career of One of Wellington's Most Highly Valued Officers in Egypt, Holland, Italy, the Peninsula and at Waterloo.

A VOICE FROM WATERLOO by *Edward Cotton*—The Personal Experiences of a British Cavalryman Who Became a Battlefield Guide and Authority on the Campaign of 1815.